Thayer L. Bancroft

D1248189

JUNGLE WAYS

by the same author

ADVENTURES IN ARABIA[1]

[1] *Published also in England and in Dutch, Swedish, and Arabic.
In preparation in French.*

THE MAGIC ISLAND[2]

[2] *Published also in England and in Czech,
French, German, Italian, Spanish, and Swedish.*

JUNGLE WAYS

BY WILLIAM B. SEABROOK

Photographs by the Author

HARCOURT, BRACE AND COMPANY

NEW YORK

Typography by Robert S. Josephy

PRINTED IN THE UNITED STATES OF AMERICA
BY QUINN & BODEN COMPANY, INC., RAHWAY, N. J.

To

PAUL MORAND

who made it possible

CONTENTS

PART ONE

FOREST PEOPLE

I

WHEN the praying mantis alighted on my hammock as we swung along the forest trail, I said to Diamoko, "It is taboo to me. Thou seest, we will not kill it, and it will tell the great serpent and the panther not to leap upon us."

He, happy, answered, "Also it will tell the tree not to fall across our path, and the river to flow mildly for our crossings."

Thus it occurred on this particular journey that Katie, who is fond of cats and was always wanting to see a panther in plain daylight, honestly never did see one.

Mori explained it otherwise. He said the outlandish uproar we made on our day marches—the singing and howling of our porters, the blaring bugle, the beating of tom-toms and blowing of ivory trumpets—scared all the animals so that they fled for their lives across the border into Liberia. It was, perhaps, an explanation, for often troops of big black apes, angry, terrified, and scolding, would go crashing westward overhead like elevated trains through the high branches.

But when we marched by torchlight, with drums and glory in the night, the wild beasts came despite the singing and sat silent with staring eyes to watch us pass.

As for our mode of travel, it resembled a wandering circus on a spree more than it did a serious white man's exploration party, but I was only following local custom, for thus the forest chiefs themselves do usually travel, and it was their own panoply they had given or lent me, supplemented by a few fantastic additions of my own.

We were in the thick of the Ivory Coast jungle, following a southward trail that ran more or less parallel with the Liberian hinterland. Motor roads, my little Citroën truck, helpful, generous French administrators, the arteries of a wide-flung colonial civilization along which one can journey with ever-increasing ease, were now left far behind. Here the blacks we encountered were still unspoiled in their unspoiled forest, and walked proudly, every man carrying either a spear, a bow and arrows, or a sword, surprised to see a white man and woman traveling with such noisy native circumstance; but always friendly, grinning so that their filed, pointed teeth showed, sometimes laughing outright, tossing jokes and compliments as we swung along.

We rode in hammock chairs, carried by naked porters

who shouted and sang continually. We always had from twenty-five to thirty of them (including headmen and song leaders), porters for hammock relays, baggage, gifts, and bar salt, which is the best gift of all. Katie's hammock was usually kept decked with bright jungle flowers, grass, and vines; mine had a scarlet-and-green plaid steamer rug draped over its lattice hood. We had drummers, dancers, players on elephant-tusk trumpets and antelope horns—and at the head of the procession marched superbly always Klon, my bugler. His name meant "the big ape." It was his family animal, and on his head he always wore a splendid wig of long black monkey fur. He went barefoot in tattered rags, but his rags clothed a tremendous pride, for they were the scraps of the uniform he had worn at Verdun, and through it showed shrapnel scars on his great ape's chest, and there was still a bit of ribbon sewn there, and the same battered brass that now echoed through the forest for our little traveling circus had sounded the charge for the Eleventh Tirailleurs at Fleury. But when peace came he had wearied of being a soldier and of the white man's country. So he had come back to his native forest and his native village, donned the family wig, gorged himself at the family pot, sacrificed to the old fetiches, and married a number of wives. But he had kept the bugle, and had become bugler for his tribal chief, fat, pompous old

Batoi at Zouan-Hounien, who had lent him to me for the trail.

I describe Klon first not merely because he marched at the head of the procession but because he was important. He had other uses in addition to the pleasure we got out of seeing him inflate his chest and the grand noises he made on the bugle. He was a good guide and pace-maker, not averse to lending a heavy hand in the camp chores at night, eager to serve Katie, and proud to aid Mori Sidi, the queer, faithful black man—it would be perhaps more accurate and gracious to say the black gentleman —who was really my chief lieutenant on this special journey. Mori was the only black among us who wore European clothes, proper, well-kept clothes of khaki, with shoes and leather puttees. He spoke and wrote clear French as well as pidjin, and had been a school-teacher. He was middle-aged, dignified, serious. He was tall, lanky, with a small, round, serious, intelligent head. Even his slightly stooped shoulders were serious. I felt that I never really learned to know him, though I trusted him, and did well to trust him. I had a feeling frequently that while he was fond of me he disapproved of me. I am accustomed to this among civilized white friends. It began with my own family in childhood. But I have felt it more rarely among so-called savages. Concerning Mori, I had suffered original misgivings because of his white schooling, his clothes, his whole association with whites, so often destructive of Negro character. But my friend Maillier, administrator at the last French post, an old colonial who knew Africa, had assured me that Mori was good, an able forest man and staunch in case of trouble.

The only other European-contacted Negro I had was Diamoko, a youth who combined the functions of cook and personal "boy." He was plump, bland, lazy, sweet-natured enough, but a terrible cook and in petty ways not to be trusted.

As for the rest of our equipment, mostly porters, they were proper good howling savages—Yafoubas—a superb, grand gang. They had their own headman, a braided-haired husky named Daa whose only garb was a leather thong round his middle and a chain diagonally across his shoulders from which dangled under his left armpit a large dead tree-rat, or rather the natural skin of one, head, tail, paws and all, which served as a bag for his private *grigris*. He carried a whip and from time to time lashed a friend in "harness" as nonchalantly as if the friend had been a horse, and the friend would accept the lash as nonchalantly. When Katie protested, they explained that it was not to punish the porters but to "encourage" them. The porters liked their headman. He was their own man. They also had a song-leader, and two or three other extras who never seemed to do any work, or in fact anything, but who were always confidently trotting along. I came to the conclusion they must be there for social companionship or because they loved traveling. I gave them the same food and wages as the others without ever asking why.

What we had, in brief, was no proper safari at all, but an intimate, noisy family that grew more intimate and noisy every mile. The porters had their traditional songs, and also were continually inventing new ones. They sang in a dialect of which I didn't then understand one syllable, but jolting along for long hours in the hammock I began trying to scribble some of the couplets phonetically, at the same time getting Mori or Diamoko to explain what they meant. There was one they often sang, accompanied by howls of laughter, which sounded something like this:

Hai yo ginga, douni yo!
Ta la tata, douni po!

I shouted to Mori, who came to walk beside my hammock, and asked him to translate. He gave ear, seemed distressed, and said, "Oh, it's just a compliment to you." I said, "Come on, Mori, what does it mean exactly? What do the words say?" He said, "Well, if you insist on my translating, it means:

8

FOREST PEOPLE

The white king is really too heavy;
The bull's back is broken;
The bull can't march any more!

From then on I bedeviled them continually for more translations, along the trail and also when we stopped to camp at night. When the porters understood what I sought, they were at first reluctant and embarrassed like children, sometimes giggling and sometimes surly like children into whose secret games a grown-up wants to poke his nose. But the results were finally well worth the trouble.

The petty chiefs and people in the villages through which we passed were welcoming us with dancing, food, drink, shelter, and good counsels, caring nothing now for the accident that my face was white, but treating me, rather, as one of their own—and for this there was a special reason quite apart from our brave, noisy native pageantry and the gifts we distributed.

Although I had not yet joined or even seen the handsome and impudent young sorceress who was later to take high-handed charge of my subsequent comings and goings in this territory, I had nevertheless faithfully followed the instructions of old Dia, the Diagbe of Loubli, who had come to me like a John the Baptist across the fields at Dananae to give me commands and

9

a leather sack full of *grigris*, in the name of his jungle gods.

These commands I had been obeying scrupulously, offering the necessary roadside sacrifices as he had taught me. Word of my doings had gone ahead on the trail, and the name by which they named me in villages which I had not yet ever entered was Mogo-Dieman, "the-black-man-who-has-a-white-face." An impatient fellow at Bounda said to a quarrelsome graybeard, "Shut up! He is older and blacker than you are."

To them, however, this was not the statement of a miracle or marvel. It was a simple fact which gave no special cause for admiration or astonishment, and certainly none for regarding me awesomely as a wonder-worker. To them no outward materialized shape is ever definite, fixed, or real. Their mysticism teaches that all outward material forms are apt to be deceptive, frequently clothing a wholly dissimilar spiritual essence. A seeming man may be a tree walking; a stone may contain the soul of one's grandfather; a child may be a serpent. Any given incarnation (materialized bodily appearance) is a transitory incident, and material forms are continually in flux. To them, therefore, my case, despite the white exterior, was commonplace and very simple. They saw me doing as they did, and not at all as other whites. I traveled in noisy pomp as a black man would,

10

drank from their calabashes, ate their food, consulted their sorcerers, obeyed their oracles, and walked softly before their gods. Therefore, very simply, I was one of them. Who knows? Perhaps Maman Célie's sorcery was still potent in me. Perhaps these blacks saw, with eyes as saints and children have for things invisible, the cross which she had traced upon my forehead.

It was after leaving Zouan-Hounien, entering the deep forest, that I began performing daily, almost hourly, the various rites and duties (most of them quite simple, naïve almost in their outward simplicity) which the Diagbe had prescribed, or rather which he had told me the forest gods demanded. He had sat naked on a mat in the twilight corner of an earth-floored hut at Dananae, with skulls and masks gazing down benevolently upon us from the shadowed walls. He had sat staring like old Ezekiel into an iron warming pan in which there was red water, and spread round it four antelope horns stuffed with herbs and blackened dung, some brass rings, his little iron serpents and crocodiles, a metal boat, and a quantity of cowrie shells, shaped and on one side blackened, so that when he tossed them on the mat like dice they made continually varied patterns. From time to time he tossed them, squeezing the horns beneath his armpits, stirring the red water, staring long into the pot.

11

Then he would say, "The Fetich commands that you do so and so."

It was these commands, thus given, that I had now begun obeying on the trail.

At a designated village we traversed on the first day's march, we halted but refused rest and hospitality (refusing even water, which the women brought for my thirsty porters), standing in the trail at the highest point among the huts. The chief and villagers gathered about us, with the customary offering of eggs, millet, and chickens, which I also refused. Following minute instructions, I seized from the forehead of a surprised hammock porter his head-ring, a tight-wound wreath of twisted leaves on which the hammock-pole rests. I laid this in the path, took off my shoes, and stood with both bare feet upon it. Diamoko brought the leather bag, also a fat live chicken from our own store. From the bag I took two kola nuts and a strip of white clean cotton cloth with which we tied the nuts beneath the chicken's wings. I said to the local chief who stood watching, "Bring me now the most miserable one in your village." He looked about in the crowd and designated a stooped old woman. I shouted angrily, "No! Here is not any charity. It concerns the Fetich." They held a hurried consultation and went away, to come back presently with a twisted paralytic whom two men carried between them like an idol and set down

like an idol on his bent, shriveled legs in front of me. I
said to him, "You will take this chicken and sacrifice it;
you will give its heart, liver, comb, and that which you
find under its right wing to the Fetich. The rest you will
eat according to your custom. That which you find under
the left wing you will keep." I spoke in pidjin and
Bambara, which Diamoko repeated in Yafouba. The
paralytic, more frightened than grateful, screamed obedi-
ence. I stepped from the porter's wreath, took it up from
the ground, walked barefooted back along the trail which
we had come, tearing the wreath in pieces and scattering
its leaves to the wind. This was my offering to the *nia*
of the air.

Klon sounded his bugle and we resumed our march.
At the first branching of the trail, the first crossroads, I
had to descend from the hammock, take off my shoes
again, put on an old pair of sandals, and walk ahead of
the porters until we came to a kola tree. At the foot of
the tree I deposited the sandals, picked up a handful of
dirt where my bare foot had touched, wrapped it in
paper, and kept it to be sewn into a leather charm. This
was my pact and plea for protection with the *nia* of the
earth.

At the first stream we forded, I tossed into a deep pool
a handsome carved bracelet which the Diagbe had provided. This was my offering to the *nia* of the rivers.

13

My offering to the *nia* of the trees, most powerful of all in the forest, required the mediation of a maiden. This was accomplished in a village where we were resting for the night. A white, new-laid egg was brought me, and in the presence of all, with Katie and me standing in their midst, I pressed it upon my forehead, upon my genitals, and then upon Katie's bared breasts, after which it was confided to the cupped hands of a naked virgin who disappeared alone into the forest to bury it secretly at the foot of a sacred tree.

I am aware that practices of this sort on the part of a supposedly enlightened white man may offer an easy butt for contemptuous smiles. I could reply with the pragmatic, cynic fact that my engaging in them inspired confidences and broke down barriers which would have otherwise remained forever closed to me, if I had lived for twenty years in Africa. (I could reply also by expressing my greater contempt, unsmiling, toward ethnologists who have never seen a living primitive "savage," but who sit at home in their studies and write about him as if he were a fossilized Etruscan or an Aztec; also toward travelers who treat him in his own country and write about him afterward as if he were a highly interesting but inferior zoölogical specimen, like a charity case, a baboon, or a penguin, and who describe his picturesque superstitions with equal condescension.) I prefer, however, to tell the truth and be damned to ridicule. Superstitious? Of course I am superstitious. I enjoyed, had pleasure and comfort doing these things, believed in their magical efficacy (spiritual if not supernatural), felt safer and more at home in the forest, doing them. Tap on wood, you others at home in New York, walk under a ladder, light three cigarettes with the same match, throw your handful of rice at the bride, and tell me that I am crazy. . . .

These were the ways of the forest, and these were the ways I followed as we went deeper and deeper into a country which became more and more mysterious with every mile. By mysterious I do not mean merely nature-mystery, the mystery which those sensitive to nature-beauty and nature-terror feel. I mean that we and all things on this trail were now surrounded by the visible signs of human sorcery, and that rules of human conduct here were controlled by the invisible forces for which these symbols stood.

Often, in bowers cut from the solid vines and foliage at the trail side, like tiny chapels or sacred niches in the vast crypt of a green cathedral, so close that we could almost touch them without swerving from the trail, were altars on which stood carven idols surrounded by votive offerings, beads, magnificent brass bracelets, sacred stones, bells, masks, objects that would enrich a village, or a

15

hungry stranger, or a thief. Yet no guardian was there, nor any accusing human eye to stay a greedy outstretched hand.

On the banks of streams where the trail crossed, stakes were planted surmounted by skulls, witch-doctor emblems, festooned with cowrie shells and necklaces more gaudy than any in my gift packs. Other votives, sometimes rich in value, sometimes mere crossed twigs or twisted bits of cloth, were hung on sacred trees.

—And not even the panther men from Liberia who crossed sometimes along these trails to raid a compound in the dead of night and carry off a child or woman slain with their iron claws, would dream of daring to touch a single bead.

Strangest of all were the curtained entrances to the mysterious, narrow "barred trails," the forbidden trails which we passed from time to time on either hand. Usually the barrier is merely a frail curtain of dried palm fiber or leaves, stretched waist-high across the simple foot-path. But no man dares to pass these barriers uninitiate. They lead to mysteries which the passer-by will never solve. They lead to the forbidden places. A twisted wisp of dried and rattling leaves which a baby hand could scatter to the wind is potent as a triple-locked steel door.

Passing at twilight, we sometimes saw processionals

emerging from these paths, ranks of young girls single file, their faces painted with white clay, led by an old woman, singing chants of coupling, fecundity, and marriage. These were the classes of newly circumcised ones (both males and females are circumcised among the Yafouba, usually after puberty), returning from the hidden sacred enclosures to sleep in their village. More rarely we encountered groups of young male initiates, their faces painted variously like weird masks, emerging with the witch-doctor from veiled trails which led to *grigris* houses where they had been undergoing instruction.

It was too early yet—my relations and my knowledge were both still insufficient—to hope for a more intimate contact with these special things. That would come later, I hoped, with friendly patience and increased understanding. Meanwhile our present objective touched on them only incidentally. Down in the forest, near the edge of the Gueré (cannibal) territory, in a village called Bin-Hounien, there was a big Yafouba chief named San Dei who lived in considerable state, and who had invited us to visit him. We had been told that we would see the so-called *jongleurs d'enfants* (magician jugglers reputed to have the power of piercing babies with their swords), masks and sculpture, dancers, snake charmers, and other marvels. They had promised elaborate preparation, and

17

we had sent runners twenty-four hours ahead of us on the trail to announce our approach.

Toward noon next day, Mori said we would probably reach Bin-Hounien in the night. We consulted the porters, and decided to go on.

When dusk came, Bugler blew a resounding fanfarrade, and we all came to a halt, strung out along the trail, while the relay porters lighted their torches, strips of dry split cane bound together in bundles, the thickness of a wrist and twice as tall as the height of a man. They crackled, gave black smoke and red leaping flame. Bugler blared another blast, the porters shouted, the drums began to boom, and we resumed our march.

Black solid forest darkness closed around us as we passed. Only where the torchlight glared directly on massed foliage, the leaves became deep, shining vivid green for an instant, then receded into total thick-walled blackness. And so we marched for hours. It was Bugler who, reaching a point where the trail hummocked to a rise, first saw lights far distant, flickering on high treetops, seeming to be moving. Half halting to give ear, we heard the drums and ivory horns and shouting of another band. The chief San Dei was on the trail to meet us. Bugler, howling with excitement like the great ape he was, came running to my hammock-side, seized my shotgun, and fired both barrels in the air. Grave, serious

Mori fired his gun too. Our porters, though wearied by a long day's march, shouting like mad, broke into a trot, and we surged forward.

Soon high-leaping naked runners appeared, brandishing their spears and torches. Their faces were blackened with charcoal, and green vines were twined over their shoulders. Five minutes later our two bands came together in a pandemonium of wild confusion. The chief San Dei, whom I had never seen before, was in a hammock like our own, but covered with a canopy of multicolored, dyed, embroidered leather, and his hammock was held high at arm's length above the heads of his porters. He was surrounded by milling dancers, girls and men, drummers and trumpeters with high plumed hats, also of colored leather, shaped like a bishop's miter. Up now went our hammocks likewise above our porters' heads. I could see my front men's muscles ripple and strain and tremble. Our hammocks were still twenty feet away from the chief's, separated by the crush. Our porters and his were fighting and pushing like bulls to bring the hammocks together, so that we jolted and swayed above the heads of the crowd.

At this moment there emerged from the shadows behind the chief's hammock a sight so extraordinary that I shouted, as excited now as any of the Negroes were, "Great God Almighty! Katie! Look!" There, higher even than we were lifted up, seeming to be walking on the mob's shoulders as one would walk miraculously on the waves in a dream, were two little black princesses, gorgeous and beautiful as an oriental fairy tale. Their slim, baby-girl bodies, standing, were naked save for glittering bracelets, anklets, jewels, but each wore a dazzling high coronet, aigrette-plumed. And each, with a tiny hand, held high a gleaming sword. As they came closer toward us above the crowd, we saw that they were standing on the shoulders of two gigantic blacks, who held their ankles tight-gripped as they swayed. The chief's headmen and mine were now laying about lustily with whips and restoring a sort of order. The baby princesses swayed closer, bowed to us solemnly; then leaning still nearer, put out their little hands to touch us on the foreheads. I learned that these were the children supposed to be pierced by swords in the magic juggling. They were treated with awe and never walked in processions or on journeys from village to village, but rode like little jockeys astride the necks and shoulders of their carriers.

The three hammocks had now been brought together and lowered. Comparative quiet was restored. We met the chief San Dei, who was to be our host. He was a big heavy man of fifty, unbearded but with a crinkly moustache, excited and perspiring, wearing heavy robes of Dioula-woven cotton, wide-striped blue and white, with store-bought tan shoes, a hat of heavy dark felt velours, also European (the furry sort which cost ten or fifteen dollars and was worn stylishly a few years ago in winter). He carried, though it was night in the dry season, an umbrella. Welcomes were exchanged, much handshaking and snapping of the fingers, more disorder as the notables of his entourage, ministers, court officials, minor dependent village chiefs, pushed eagerly forward to see our faces and shake hands too.

With Mori interpreting and explaining, we learned from San Dei that (after consultation with his witch-doctors, who knew the sanctions under which I traveled) he had decided, instead of putting us in the public guest house in his village on the main trail, to take us directly to his smaller private ancestral village which was situate at the end of a branch trail, an hour westward toward the Liberian border. And thus it was agreed.

So we formed a noisy, disordered merged processional, and with a mighty howling that finally became rhythmic with the trumpets and the drums, moved forward in the red glare of waving torches and black shadows. First went the chief's naked, leaping runners; then Bugler, sounding now and then a blast that shrilled golden above the rhythmic tumult; then the baby princesses astride their human horses, followed by the tomtom beaters and plumed trumpeters, by girls, high-breasted, beautiful, and old hags dancing; then our swaying hammocks followed by the crowd. . . .

And suddenly it became too much for me. It was too much glory for the ears, and too much glory for the eyes, in the torchlight with the waving spears.

We had turned off the main trail into one so narrow that it was like a dream-passage through solid green rock cliffs which opened, swaying away like branches, and then closed in again impenetrable.

So presently, tired and as if still in a dream, we came to the ancestral village—peaked, thatched roofs rising clustered from circular, low mud walls—and soon we lay alone in our camp beds beneath one of the roofs, grateful for darkness and silence, too tired for anything but sleep.

II

IT WAS grave-faced Mori who came discreetly to
arouse us in the guest house from a sleep so sound
that we blinked our eyes and only really awakened
when we heard Bugler, the Great Ape, just outside our
door, bugling God knows what with a blare that would
raise the dead. Free now from corporals and sergeants,
back in his own jungle, he was a child with a superb
toy, and sounded indiscriminately mess-calls, reveilles,
charges, taps, retreats, intermingled with fanfarrades of
his own personal invention, whenever and wherever it
suited his own fine fancy free.

Mori announced that San Dei, our host, the tribal
chief, was coming to visit us as soon as we were ready
to receive him. Straw mats were laid outside our door
while we dressed and had coffee. Aided by Diamoko and
Bugler, Mori contrived a table and found chairs for us.
While awaiting the chief's visit we sat, smoked cigarettes,
and looked about us on a new little world, for arriving
tired, late the night before, we had seen almost nothing.

23

We were in the midst of a small village, tight closed in by forest, some thirty houses built in irregular concentric circles around a large central clearing of bare, hard earth. In the middle of this central clearing stood a single tree with wide-spreading branches, under which were mats and benches. There was a big monkey free in the tree, now playing from branch to branch in the morning sun —not sacred or totemistic, I learned, but simply a village pet. Most of the houses, like the one in which we lodged, were circular and small, about twenty feet in diameter, mud walls rising waist-high only, surmounted by peaked roofs of grass. One had to crouch, almost on all fours, to enter by the single door, and there were no windows. However, there were two very large rectangular houses, facing the clearing as ours did, but with higher doorways and mat-curtained windows indicating a number of chambers. One evidently was the chief's. The other, apparently, was closed up and empty. I wondered casually why he hadn't given us that to lodge in, since he was so hospitably planning to upset the whole village for our pleasure.

Now he emerged from his own house and came across the clearing, pompous but cordial and friendly, to offer us good morning. He was dressed as the night before, and still carried the umbrella, folded. He was accompanied by his counselors, followed by servants who brought the

usual gifts of live chickens, eggs, rice, fruit, kola nuts,
palm wine in calabashes. Another servant carried his
chair, and another a horse's-tail fly-swatter with a silver
handle. We shook hands in the Yafouba manner, which
is like our own except that you break the grip with a
smart jerk, snapping your fingers at the instant of the
break, with the force communicated by the let-go. I
had learned to do it not too badly. San Dei sat down
with us at table, still pompous but cordial, a combina-
tion difficult to sustain. The several notables of his entourage, some graybeards and some younger, some robed
and some naked save for their loin-cloths and leather
grigris, sat round us on the mats. Among the robed ones
was a nephew of the chief, a man of perhaps thirty,
named Yo. There seemed something special about him,
something indefinitely but immediately sensed which
made me vaguely feel him different from the others. He
had a kindly, intelligent, young bearded face, and as I
watched him it seemed to me that there was a sort of
contained sadness in his eyes. Nor did I misread his face
or imagine this, though I learned the reason for it only
later. I was concerned just now in making a proper impression on San Dei.

All African chiefs love ceremonies, and I had invented
a modest little ceremonial for such occasions. I had
bought in Paris and had carefully packed singly against

breakage a number of good Japanese porcelain cups and saucers, decorated in bright colors with figures of Japanese ladies, landscapes, and dragons. Mori now brought one of these teacups with its saucer, which he unpacked and placed on the table. Beside it we put two ordinary white-enameled mugs from the camp-kit. Likewise a bottle of sweet sparkling wine, which I opened, letting the cork pop into the air, and poured some of it bubbling into the teacup. I would taste first from it, in conformity with forest etiquette, then Katie would taste, then the chief, and after having drunk he would keep it as a memento. So we did solemnly, then finished the bottle, he drinking most of it from the teacup, we drinking from the common ones. I had not called his attention to the ladies, trees, and dragons. He found them for himself, turning the fragile cup not clumsily in his thick black hands. I showed him how to hold it against the light so the images would appear through the translucent porcelain. Then we all drank some of his banghi in a calabash bowl brass-studded, but only a little for ceremony, since it was early in the morning, and I presented him with a hunting-knife.

While our breakfast was cooking, we strolled with San Dei, visiting the village. It was like any Yafouba cluster, except that it had the two great houses instead of one. I noticed now that the chief's house was quite new. They explained that the second great house, closed and silent, was that of his dead elder brother, Bou, the former tribal chief, deceased only five months past. Bou's tomb which they would presently show me was in a garagelike shed beside the great house, built lightly of bamboo poles and thatching. Close behind it were grouped the houses of Bou's former wives, eight of them, young and old, who had become the property of his son Yo (San Dei's nephew), who was walking with us. We paid the wives a visit. They were working harmoniously at their household tasks, helping each other like sisters in the common yard where iron pots were simmering and manioc was being pounded in wooden mortars with tall poles for pestles. One wife was nursing a posthumous baby begotten by the old dead chief, and two were pregnant by his son, their present master. Thus family life went on. Although still wives, as well as widows, their heads were all close-shaven, young and old, and their faces smeared with yellow clay. A pregnant one and two others wore the handsome, enormous brass anklets, seen only in this part of the forest, and worn here only by special "favorite wives." Such anklets, worn always in pairs, weigh frequently twelve to fifteen pounds each and measure eight to ten inches in diameter. They are forged on the young bride by the blacksmith, and worn for life. She is exempt from harder forms of labor, like a Chinese lady with bound feet, and immensely proud. She learns to walk freely, even dance in them. She is fettered heavily, yet free. The effect is not without a certain barbarous sadistic magnificence.

Our visit finished with the wives, San Dei took me to see his brother's tomb. It was a simple mound, but stained with the black, dry blood of recent sacrifices; around it on the walls hung masks and images, leather *grigris* bags ornamented with panther teeth and claws. There was no secrecy here, nor about the silent great house either, which we next visited. Its doors were closed, but not locked or fastened. They merely asked me not to touch or displace anything. The furniture and intimate personal belongings of the old chief were dust-covered, but otherwise as if he had left them only yesterday for a short journey. One felt that he might return at any moment. They told me that as a matter of fact he often did. For a year, or perhaps longer, everything would remain undisturbed so that the chief's *nia* (a sort of disembodied personal essence more like ghost than soul) could come and go at will and find his couch, his umbrella, his favorite belongings in their accustomed places. No human being would ever dwell in the house again. Later, when the witch-doctors decided, it would be burned as the other homes of ancestral chiefs had been burned before it.

When we emerged from this ghost-inhabited gray silence into the sunshine, we found the village seething with preparations for the fête. Bands of drummers, dancers, jugglers, masked mummers, and musicians, summoned from miles around and followed by their own village groups, were assembling in the big compound. We pushed our way through them, returned to our hut, ate hastily, and then rejoined San Dei beneath the shade of the tree. We sat with him on the benches, our entourage grouped standing behind. The entire compound was massed with excited spectators, nearly an acre of them. Immediately in front of us, a space about twice the size of a prize-fight ring was kept clear. The musicians and entertainers, many of them masked or painted, were seated in a semicircle waiting their turns, and behind them men with staves and little whips held the crowd back.

First appeared the *griots*. These are a special class, and divide further into two separate specialized functions. One type of *griot* is like the subsidized poet or minstrel who was attached to a European court in the Middle Ages. He is an improvising singer, shouter, orator, whose duty is to flatter and glorify his master. The second type of *griot* corresponds even more precisely to the mediaeval king's jester. He is a comic fellow to whom ever outrageous license is permitted. Every important Ivory Coast chief has one or more of each of these types attached to his train.

San Dei's prize shouting-singer now stood before us, an elderly man, robed, with shaven head. He bowed profoundly and with dignity, then leaped high into the air like a jumping-jack, emitting a series of wild yells to gain the attention of the crowd. Pointing to San Dei, he shouted at the top of his voice:

Behold, the mountain is always in its place!
He is the man of men!
He is the husband [protector] of all the young men!
He is the Great Warrior, and when he goes to battle only
  one man is left alive in the ruined village!
He is like his father and his grandfather;
When people speak of him behind his back in whispers,
He comes shouting and makes them all beg for mercy.
He is a bitter tree, well rooted;
You can't pull him up with your teeth.
He is Douma, the Great Thunder!

The orator who had been punctuating each of these separate strophes with wild yells, in which the crowd joined, now paused for breath, and well he might. In this pause a divertissement occurred spontaneously which gave me considerable delight. My erstwhile pompous though friendly host, San Dei, had been getting more and more excited, perspiring and puffing with his own grandeur. Now, unable longer to contain himself on the bench beside us, he arose ponderously waving his umbrella, and let out a wild howl all his own. Brandishing the umbrella like a spear or war-club, he began strutting before us, exciting himself still further until what had begun as a strut ended in unwieldy caperings, while he shouted:

"Yes! Yes! It is true! I am the great one! I am an elephant! I am the strongest! I am the man of men! I am the great warrior! I am indeed a bitter tree! Ho! Ho! Wow! Behold me!"

He sat down puffing, and we all congratulated him heartily. A second *griot* now turned his attention to me, but he sang rather than shouted, and four others stood behind him who hummed a harmonious accompaniment as when glee-club singers imitate guitars. It was very nice. He first sang:

> *When the bird flies,*
> *It notifies nobody*
> *And carries neither heavy baggage*
> *Nor royal gifts.*
> *But when a king comes,*
> *Behold, it is not the same.*

He then sang:

When I first beheld you,
I was astonished
And said, "What is this?"
But when I looked more closely,
It was as if I looked upon my father's face.

The song he sang which I liked best was this:

> *When you came along the hard trail*
> *Through the forest,*
> *The panthers fled in fear.*
> *But the little goats came down,*
> *Bleating from the rocks,*
> *To watch you pass.*

Then turning to the crowd like a football cheer-leader, he shouted:

"Who is here?

"He is here!

"The one who always conquers."

The crowd assented, shouting it after him joyfully. I was very proud, happy, and flattered. I gave him two bars of salt and my pocket-knife.

Now a comic *griot* appeared, an old man grimacing, naked but for a ridiculous feathered loincloth, who seized San Dei's umbrella, snatched the hat off his head, then began mimicking him, strutting and shouting:

"I am indeed the loud noise! Yow! Wow! Hoho! B-r-r-oooom! I am an elephant! That is to say, I am the hind parts of an elephant! Hear the great thunder!"

After which he came and sat down in the chief's chair —that is, on top of the chief—bouncing up in surprise like one who has sat down on a cat when San Dei cuffed his ears.

Turning to me, he snatched my helmet as he had the chief's hat, put it on his own head, demanded my thumb ring, then began going through all my pockets like a monkey, taking everything he found, even including my wallet and handkerchief. Capering about, he showed them to the crowd, and then restored them, all but the helmet. He went over to Katie, pushing her half off the bench to sit down beside her, putting his arms around her, hugging her like a bear, pantomiming, pretending to be me, her husband. He took her necklace of turquoise beads, her hand-bag, even her two diamond rings, running away and capering in the crowd, as he had with my belongings. Then he rushed back, patted us, fondled us, exhibited us, proud and pleased we had trusted him.

Next came two masked dancers. Their masks (good Ivory Coast wood-carving) were set in immense head-dresses, ornamented with bells and plumes, fur, panther teeth, and shells, which hooded their entire heads and shoulders. Long sleeves of cloth, sewn up like bags, covered their arms and hands. Their bodies, all but the bare feet, were hidden by heavy, flaring skirts of woven grass. Both were men, but one wore the mask of a female witch, the other that of a devil-animal. They danced a sexual dance, a sort of jungle witch's sabbath, in which the staff held by the latter served the rôle of a monstrous phallus.

A snake charmer followed. He had two cobras in a wooden box. He made them coil, hiss, spread their hoods, and strike, according to his will, singing and talking to them. He had no flute or musical instrument, but with his voice he could keep them swaying. He made them follow him about, climb on his body, coil round his neck, spread their hoods there, swaying, and put their heads in his mouth. Their ugly fangs were still intact. He also assured us, of course, that they were still deadly, but whether or not he had removed their poison glands, we had no way of telling.

Various groups of dancers now succeeded. Men with spears did the dance of killing a panther; others did the stealthy dance of hunting apes with bow and arrow; girls loaded with clinking bracelets and belled anklets did sexual dances until they fell panting, exhausted as if from actual coupling; a band of girls, highly stylized in a ballet without stage props, pantomimed village, field, and household tasks, digging roots, picking bananas, gathering wood, fetching water, lighting fire, pounding millet. For the climax of this ballet, one girl became a chicken, and fled squawking, flapping wings. The others chased it, shooed it, cornered it, and pretended to wring its neck. Then it bounced and fluttered and somersaulted in the dust as a wrung-necked chicken does, while the crowd howled with laughter and applause. Four handsome youths appeared, braceleted, ankleted, loaded with beads, their elaborate coiffures stuck through with long aluminum and wooden hairpins. They were female impersonators. They postured, danced, and wriggled with a lascivious abandon which made me wonder whether they were not actual androgynes. I was told they were simple pantomime artists like the rest.

All this, however, was but a preparation, a "curtain-raising" for the principal event—the sword jugglers with their baby girls. They had been in seclusion, at the other end of the village, in the witch-doctors' enclosure. A lane was made for their triumphant entry through the crowd. The girls rode astride the necks of the same giants who had carried them to meet us on the trail. But before them marched two gorillalike men whom I had never seen before—gorillas not in the sense that they were bestial or repulsive, but by the tremendous development of their chests, arms, and shoulders, beautiful muscularly but almost monstrous, so that they seemed foreshortened,

35

stocky, though of normal height. These were the jugglers.

Before the performance began, the baby girls were "magically" immunized. A thick, dark, dryish paste from a horn bottle was smeared lightly on their foreheads, palms, and breasts, while in the complete silence which had now fallen the two jugglers muttered their mumbo-jumbo. The babies, they said, were to be pierced, impaled upon the swords, before our eyes.

A brilliant exhibition followed, transparent Coney Island balderdash as magic—mere legerdemain and optical illusion, but lifted high above banality by such daring jugglery as only a people holding life lightly would risk with little children. The two gorillalike men, standing first ten, then nearly twenty, feet apart, and using the babies as human projectiles, began "warming up" like basketball champions. They hurled them back and forth in parabola, now curled into balls like sleeping porcupines, now cart-wheeling through the air with arms and legs spread wide, now rigid, straight, headlong, like torpedoes shot from a tube. The two baby girls had become passive like rag-dolls, somnolent and relaxed as if hypnotized, and I wondered if they were. In the pauses they stood with eyes wide open which seemed to see nothing, and their faces were as expressionless as if carved in wood. The jugglers rested, breathing heavily, and then began the sword-play. One held two swords straight out before him, rigid at arm's length, aimed slightly upward, glittering, sharp-edged and sharp-pointed. From a distance of fifteen feet the other hurled a child upon the sword points. It flashed sidewise in an arc, directly, it seemed, upon the points of the unlowered blades, which seemed in that fraction of an instant to be piercing it through and through. But a fraction of an instant later the body lay unharmed, caught in the cupped elbows of the juggler. This brilliant trick, almost convincing to a credulous eye, was repeated in numerous variations with both the little girls, who remained always wooden-faced and passive. The exhibition was over. The crowd applauded violently and I applauded too, but I was a little disappointed.

It had been thrilling, but it wasn't "stage magic" of this sort, even at its finest, that I had come seeking in West Central Africa.

I said as much candidly afterward to Mori and San Dei, and got something in return for my candor. San Dei said, "I was willing but my witch-doctors were not. They were afraid that evil might befall if it were performed in the face of strangers."

I said, "If what were performed?"

He replied, "There is real magic; children are pierced and carried with the swords run through their bodies, but it is very dangerous. The recovery does not always take place. It is perhaps better that it was not attempted."

I am relating this conversation because a month later I returned to Bin-Hounien and saw disturbing things which I will describe when I tell of that return, but for which I can offer no adequate explanation.

The sequel of the present exhibition, however, was innocent and charming. Katie and I were in our hut in the late afternoon, half napping, lying together on a floor mat where it was cooler than in our camp beds. With eyes half closed I became conscious that some one was entering the hut. Standing just inside the doorway, hand in hand like any kids, were the two tiny girls, washed and prettied, smiling. Squatting outside the door were the two jugglers who had brought them, and who grinned and beamed benevolently. The children, fearless, friendly, full of curiosity, cuddled down like kittens on the mat beside us, sucked lumps of sugar which we gave them, played with Katie's beads, examined her hair and clothes with their fingers, then spied a pair of her slippers. Each put on one of them, laughing and hopping about. We gave them each a pearl necklace and a strip of blue cloth, also a little bottle of perfumery, sprinkling a few drops on their palms to show them its use. They were as sweet and clean as any white baby-girls fresh from a tub.

After they and the jugglers had gone away with their gifts, we dined in the twilight before our hut. Chicken

and omelettes which Diamoko had prepared were supplemented by a great bowl of goat liver and rice sent by the
chief. Presently, after darkness had fallen, Mori came
to say that I was awaited to take part in the banghi
drinking of the notables on the thatch-canopied porch
of San Dei's house where torches had already been
planted.

Mori brought my chair, San Dei had his own, and
the others sat on grass mats. The banghi had already
been brought, in big calabash bottles holding a couple
of gallons each, wicker-wound and wicker-handled like
Chianti flasks, with little tubelike spouts of changeable
fresh green palm leaf. We drank from calabash bowls,
filled brimming, which held almost a quart for a
draught. The pourers, who were servants, always drank
first from each newly broached bottle, and sipped also
from each poured bowl before it was offered. Soon several bowls were circulating. It was good palm wine,
milky opaque, well fermented, heady, and not too sweet.
When one has drunk a gallon or so of it, one becomes
merry, exuberant, and slightly wobbly on the feet. One
pays extravagant mutual compliments, one boasts in a
friendly way, and one is easily induced to sing. San
Dei led presently a Yafouba war song, which put it into
my head to sing "John Brown's Body." I tried, through
Mori, to explain the words. They understood very well,

39

for they all believe that when a man lies moldering his soul goes marching on. But this seemed a bit too serious, and the bawdy urge came upon me, as it often does when slightly in my cups, to sing "Columbo." San Dei patted me on the back and said it was a fine song.

I was happy, full of friendliness, slightly sentimental, and (in a vague sort of way which is difficult to put in words) indifferent to the geographical fact that this was so-called savage Africa. I was glad to be there. It was a good place to be. It was a good drinking party. It seemed as natural and simple to be there as in the up-stairs room of the Brasserie de l'Odéon at Paris or in some friendly speakeasy in New York.

But an episode presently occurred (the blame entirely mine) which destroyed my overconfident illusion that all was sweetness and light and everybody simple and happy as myself. Nothing is ever simple, anywhere. Among us sat the young bearded nephew of San Dei, the young robed chief named Yo, whose eyes had seemed vaguely sad when we first met. He seemed vaguely sad still, and I had begun to notice that he was the only one who was not drinking. I am very much ashamed of what I did, for it was stupid. It was the kind of expansive, good-hearted effort to patronize which I loathe in any man, and of which I am sometimes guilty. I had a sudden surge of brotherly love for Yo and an idea that

40

he was being neglected. So I tried with friendly, insistent, blatant ostentation to force a bowl on him. I tried to make a man drink who politely didn't want to and who refused politely. Every one was embarrassed but me. Finally Mori, grave-faced, worried, almost angry, shook me by the shoulder and whispered in my ear:

"Please stop. I beg you. You do not understand. This man is to be poisoned."

He said it as if he were explaining a fact static, unhurried, yet inevitable—as if he were saying, "You mustn't urge this man to drink, because he has Bright's disease." If Mori had said, "This man is afraid of being poisoned," or "He knows somebody is going to try to poison him," it would have been more natural, and easy of comprehension. But there was something in what he actually said, and in the way he said it, which took it outside and beyond white psychology, just as there was something beyond white comprehension in the way Yo sat there, sad-faced and knowing, yet talking and even smiling from time to time, among his friends and family. Here was an accepted future fact. It would not occur that night, perhaps not for many nights. But it would arrive in its destined time like the changing season or the waning of the moon. There was fate in it, as if from no primary human volition. And there was no escape.

All this I sensed, and it sobered me and left me won-

41

dering. I had, curiously, no precise feeling of pity toward Yo, and certainly no silly, futile thought that I might help him. It was all passing in a dark realm where my pities and values held no meaning and into which I had blindly blundered. I felt that I should have in some way begged humbly all their pardons.

When Mori took me home to the hut where Katie lay already asleep, we sat for a long time outside the door and he told me what he knew of the recent tribal history, reproaching himself that he had not told me sooner.

Here then briefly was the tale of San Dei's family and succession, the invisible drama with its last act written but yet unplayed, which was moving to its climax in this hidden forest village where we two whites had been received with generous hospitality and happy festival:

More than a year before, the old chief, Bou, San Dei's brother, whose body lay dead over there in its bamboo mausoleum and whose unrevengeful ghost dwelt honored in the darkened great house, had begun to weaken and lose his power. San Dei had already become in reality the tribal leader, the power behind the tottering throne. There had been a conference of witch-doctors and ministers which had resulted in the poisoning of the old chief. According to Mori's understanding, it had not been an act dictated by ambition or jealousy on San Dei's part, any more than the projected poisoning of the old chief's

42

son would be. It had been a measure for the collective tribal good, to which the individual is always sacrificed when need be. Circumstances now made it seem necessary to remove Yo in the same way. It was not that he had been making trouble or fomenting any secret plot to overthrow San Dei. It was rather that as the old chief's son, and not a weakling, he might become the center of a movement to upset the balance under which the tribe was prospering. No promise, or good will, or present loyalty on his part could guarantee against this possibility, for the blacks believe, as the classic Greeks did, that a man may be driven to engage in such acts by occult forces wholly outside his own intention or volition. Up to this point one might find abundant parallels, and worse, in the dubious history of our own white royal houses. What seemed to me more curious, and perhaps without exact parallel among us, was that the intended victim, Yo, fully cognizant of what awaited him, made no effort toward ultimate defense or escape, but remained there with the tribe, and with the very family, apparently unresentful, doing nothing to protect himself beyond the futile temporary gesture of not drinking freely with the others. He could easily have fled to another tribe, or into Liberia, or even to a French administration post. Mori explained his remaining as a sort of tribal duty. It was his duty for the collective tribal good to

43

remain passively and be poisoned. It seemed to me a duty which the noblest white altruist would scarcely have regarded as imperative. True, we hold that it is heroic and beautiful *(dulce et decorum est)* to die for others. "Greater love hath no man," we repeat. But I think our purest-hearted voluntary victims expect a *positive* posthumous run of some sort for their spiritual money. I doubt whether even a Socrates or Joan of Arc would sit about, placidly awaiting the stake or hemlock, for the purely negative reason that they might be in the way later; or whether any white group short of Plato's imaginary Utopian republic would inflict death without a qualm for so negative a reason. I caught myself wondering whether the Negro was simply more indifferent to life, or whether he was going both us and Plato one better in beautiful selflessness. . . .

At any rate, I felt myself totally incapable of forming a gratuitous judgement either on the passively waiting victim or those who were concocting his demise. It seemed to be a family, village, tribal matter, settled in advance to everybody's satisfaction. When San Dei came to take me hunting next morning, there was Yo beside him, coming along too. Everything was just as if I hadn't stumbled the night before into a dark room from which Mori had dragged me before I went too far. San Dei was our hospitable host for three more days. When we departed, returning toward Dananae, he gave us a number of masks, and Yo gave Katie an otter pelt softly tanned, pliable as a glove. On the farewell morning they accompanied us to the main trail and insisted on lending us additional porters for our first day's march.

III

Two weeks had elapsed since our first adventure among the Yafouba. Katie I had seen comfortably installed at Man, a French administration post in the mountains, where she had house and servants, car and chauffeur. Man was deep in the forest—a native town with everything built of mud and thatching, including the administration buildings—but connected with the coast by motor road, post, and telegraph. It was to be our base during the Ivory Coast sojourn.

As for me, I was back again at Dananae, seated again on a mat in the Diagbe's hut, with his masks and skulls grinning down on us as we palavered far into the night. Mori had rejoined me and we were planning a longer trail excursion, perhaps into Liberia. I was trying to persuade the Diagbe himself to accompany us. He was protesting that he was too old and feeble. I was disappointed, for experience had convinced me that my only hope of penetrating deeper beneath surface things lay in traveling sponsored by the actual presence of some one who had intimate, authoritative contact with the depths.

46

In short, I had conceived the presumptuous but practical notion that, having acquired my own bugler, beaters on tomtoms, and shouters, I must now acquire a private witch-doctor. Mori thought (as he often did) that I was crazy. But the old Diagbe was sympathetic.

After pondering awhile, he said: "No, I cannot do it. But I have a cousin, younger, it is true, but known and powerful, who travels widely and who may be persuaded to make the journey, if the Fetich is favorable. Come back tomorrow morning and we shall see."

What we saw when we reëntered the Diagbe's hut next morning was by no means what I had bargained for. There was no sign of a second witch-doctor, but seated cross-legged beside the Diagbe was a handsome, youngish female creature, scantily garbed, in a red leather hat with feathers, who fanned herself nonchalantly with a silver-handled cow's tail, and contemplated me with a bland, disturbing smile.

"But where is your cousin?" I demanded of the Diagbe.

"But here is my cousin," he replied. "She is willing to go with you—in a hammock—if the signs are favorable, but the Fetich must be consulted first. . . ."

"—*Non*," interrupted Mori hastily in French, "*pas ça, monsieur, je vous en prie.*"

"Why not?" I said. "If she is a real witch-doctor"—

but this was partly bravado. If she had been old and ugly, or at least wrinkled as a proper sorceress ought to be, I should have felt on safer ground.

"She is a real sorceress," he said. "The Diagbe has trained her from childhood, and her power is known in the forest. But it isn't that. I have never seen her before, but I know her reputation. As a woman, when not concerned with her Fetich, she is impudent as a monkey, hard-headed as a goat, and a comedian on top of it."

This was not reassuring, but I found myself pushed along, without time for reflection, perhaps out of sheer perversity to plague solemn Mori. I told him his description fitted all females whether white or black, saints or sorceresses, and that I proposed to do whatever the Fetich decided.

So the paraphernalia was made ready and the invocation began. The Diagbe, kneeling, placed a pierced calabash seed between his teeth, with which he made a weird, whistling drone. It was rhythmic and sounded curiously like Lilliputian bagpipes far away. The woman sat cross-legged before him, swaying. After a time she began to breathe heavily. The swaying ceased and she sat shuddering as if shaken by a galvanic current. The expression of her face had changed. The wide-awake, keen impudence was gone. She sat staring, a black sibyl rather beautiful. The shuddering ceased, and even before

48

I knew what form the test would take, I had the impression that her body had become like a battery, tensioned, highly charged. In her hands were two polished antelope horns. These she now pressed against her shoulders, in the hollow above the armpits, where they adhered. She shook herself, and they still adhered. She put out her two hands and seized mine in a tight grip. It may easily have been my imagination which made it seem that a sort of current flowed into my fingers. But when the Diagbe laid two short, heavy ivory wands on my forearms, they adhered like the horns on the woman's shoulders. She shook my arms violently and the wands did not fall. This, the Diagbe said, was a sign that the Fetich was favorable. She let go my hands and the wands dropped immediately to the ground. Tricks, of course, or not, as you choose. But nothing so simple as stickum or vacuum adhesion. My own opinion concerning such phenomena, which primitive *illuminés* frequently produce and do not themselves regard as particularly extraordinary, is that they may possess through strong emotion-concentration a practical control over physiological dynamic forces, perhaps merely electro-chemical, which our own advanced science recognizes in theory but has not yet put to practice. I have wondered sometimes, pure speculation, whether primitive sorcery (and esoteric black magic) may not possess also a control, more important to know about, over certain aspects of the fourth-dimensional world, equally recognized in our new time-space theories since Einstein. If this were true, of course, it could explain phenomena of a heavier and more baffling category without the gratuitous blanket assumption of trickery or the necessity of crying miracle.

While I was speculating, the young sorceress had emerged from her abnormal state, still serious. She said she had seen trouble on the trail, obstacles, disappointments for me and trouble for her, but that the Fetich had told her to go with me and that she would go. She seemed a different sort of woman now, and I wondered whether my first impression had been wrong. I was to learn that this Wamba was in fact two sorts of woman; spoiled and high-handed, an impudent comedian, as Mori had said, a luxurious young she-devil who would have been the better off for a good beating; yet a true *illuminée*, a true abnormal, a black sorceress in very truth, whom the natives recognized and feared.

However, meanwhile (since the Negroes had all been treating me as a sort of friendly chief if not a master), I had fallen into the habit of commanding, and felt that in a sense, I was "employing" a sorceress as I had employed my lieutenant Mori, Bugler, and other principals of our traveling circus. So I said authoritatively, "We will start at dawn then, tomorrow morning."

"Oh, no, we won't," said Wamba. "We will start on tomorrow's morrow, if I can get ready."

It was clear who intended to be the important one and give orders from then on, but though I am never really much good at commanding, I wasn't ready to establish precedent quite so easily for a whim. I knew she could have got ready in ten minutes if she had wished. I said a bit truculently, "Did the Fetich tell you you must wait?" She laughed and said, "No. But I have a circumcision class at Flambli which I must visit tomorrow. . . ."

One plans, one studies, one works hard to make things happen, one goes on long useless journeys to find something, but it is almost always by the side issue of pure chance—luck—that one arrives anywhere. I said, "Your cousin, the Diagbe here, knows that I respect the forest ways and perform the rites. I suppose he has already told you this. In his presence now I ask you to let me go with you tomorrow, if it is not forbidden. If you can let me go with you, I will give you something very pretty." I had expected hesitancy, probable refusal. Instead, they agreed quite simply.

So next morning it came to pass, by this good fortune's casual hazard, that sponsored by my sorceress, we parted curtain barriers of dried grass and walked the veiled, forbidden paths. We walked indeed for several long kilometers in the morning's forest coolness, and came finally to a frail bamboo stockade whose entrance was barred only by another light grass curtain. But at the right of the entrance stood a brave little wooden man with an enormous phallus painted red, and at its left a little wooden woman with an equally emphasized vagina. Here in this forest sacred college, young maidens, brides-to-be, spared nonsense of storks and cabbage-heads, were instructed in what the Rev. Dr. Sylvanus Stall calls in his quaint, mildly pornographic volumes, "the sacred facts of life."

Wamba shouted to announce us, and we entered the enclosure. It was a pleasant fenced clearing, with shade trees left standing, and a thatched peristyle. Pots, calabashes, mortars for pounding grain, were scattered about; piles of colored pebbles, dropped hastily, with which forest children play a game like jackstones, and wooden boards with scooped depressions on which they play a game somewhat like checkers. It was a rather lovely scene, not at all weird or solemn. It was more like the interrupted picnic of a girls' boarding-school. The girls themselves—there were nine of them, budding young females who would soon become wives—stood in a dutiful row to receive their mistress, then knelt with their foreheads pressed against the ground. Their faces were painted chalk white, and they wore many bracelets of brass and aluminum, gifts of their future husbands. One of the girls, who was of the class but seemed to be a sort of monitor, had a chain crosswise over her shoulders, from which hung a horn bottle. I asked if it was *grigris*. Not exactly, explained Wamba; it was medicament. I could examine it if I wished. It was a gray, pasty mess, with an odor that was strong but not unpleasant. It contained ashes, she said, red pepper, grease, and a number of healing herbs. It stung sharply, but prevented infection. The circumcision ceremony had been performed three weeks before, and the class was now almost ready to be dismissed. I began asking her questions about the mechanics of the operation. What did she do it with? She searched in her leather bag to show me, and produced a Gillette safety razor blade to which a small wooden handle had been added. Formerly they used an iron knife, she said, but this was better. Where did she get it? All the Dioulas (black Mohammedan pack peddlers from the Soudan) sold them.

There was another mechanical point on which I wanted information. Ethnologists have denounced this custom of female circumcision, asserting (on hearsay) that in the operation among the West Coast people, the clitoris is excised—which seemed a fine example of learned ethnographic nonsense. Wamba couldn't at first even understand what I meant. Then, with the utmost simplicity in

53

the world, she selected one of the girls at random and showed me. The operation was almost completely healed, and had consisted solely of excising the surplus folds inside the lips of the vagina—a measure which had become ritual like all things connected with the mating function, but must certainly have had as its basic purpose common-sense facility for cleanliness, just as in the case of male circumcision.

I was a bit surprised to learn (not because they were Negroes but because they were primitives living under somewhat difficult sanitary conditions) that their sexual hygiene was admirable in other respects as well. Wamba showed me a sort of syringe made from a long-handled gourd, shaped like the ordinary glass retort, long-spout-and-globe, which one sees in a chemical laboratory. This syringe is filled with warm water and medicament, and is operated by blowing hard through a little round hole in the top of the globe. Similar devices, with a piston for air-pressure, were common in Europe before the invention of the whirling spray. Every decent Yafouba household, Wamba said, possessed one.

She told me I must now wait outside the enclosure while some woman's religious rite was performed that males were forbidden to see. Without meaning to eavesdrop I heard them droning their chants in unison, and walked farther down the trail until I was out of hearing.

When she rejoined me, I asked what else the girls did there all day, for three mortal weeks, from dawn to twilight. She laughed and said, "Mostly they make nonsense. Most of the time they play their games, frolic, and make up funny stories. They must learn certain things of course, make their sacrifices, and cook, but most of the time they make nonsense."

I thought this was all splendid, even if it wasn't as weird and solemn as I had expected. Also I began to be very glad that Wamba had agreed to accompany us on the long trail.

We started the next morning. Bugler, notified in advance, had collected porters and brought them to Dananae. Wamba had her own hammock—not a heavy chair swung between poles like mine, but a net hammock with a single long pole, in which she lazed like Cleopatra and lorded it reclining. I supplied her porters. She traveled without any baggage save her sack of *grigris* and her cow's tail scepter. Whatever she needed, or fancied, she demanded and took. Whether on the trail or in camp, she respected none of my possessions or my privacies. She even had the impudence to insist on the gift of my thumb ring with its Gnostic seal which I wouldn't part with for a wilderness of witches. This was not cupidity. It was the little intaglio god with a panther's head that attracted her. We compromised by my letting her wear it a part of the time. She told the others I had given it to her. It had never occurred to Mori, much less Bugler, however friendly, to make common pot with me—not because I was white but because I was chief; they provided their own food, according to custom. Wamba sat at table with me, was served by Diamoko, and beat him as I would have never dared when she didn't like his cooking. On the very first night she had spread her mat beside me, and before morning, naturally, she was in my bed. Since the folding camp bed was too narrow (and a continual nuisance anyway) we dispensed with it and slept thereafter together on the mat in native fashion.

But Wamba's presence in our caravan was not all dalliance and comedy by any means. Villages through which we passed knew her of old, recognized and feared her. We had a prestige less noisy but more serious than on the former journey.

The night before we started, she had taken me alone into a mud swamp near the river where we had buried a bottle containing oil, water, palm wine, and the blood of a cock which she killed there and whose entrails she examined with great care. Muttering her incantations in the moonlight, she was not funny. She was on the job.

I have said that with Wamba I seemed to be dealing with two women rather than one, but I think in reality, absurd as it may appear to present an African jungle witch in such paradoxical guise, that she was not only a true sorceress but a true Negress, true to type and true to the genius of her race—light-minded, sensual, a luxurious pleasure-loving animal, comic at times, gaily insolent, yet good-hearted—but with another side, another soul, dark and primordial, in continual unconscious deep communication with old nameless things, demoniac and holy.

Because I felt this about the woman, or perhaps simply because I was beginning to enjoy her, I endured Wamba's whims and obeyed her as we journeyed southward, unhurried, entertained in various villages. I was rewarded well. We performed in a witch-doctor's house at Glangleu the somewhat unpleasant marassa mystery whose beginnings I had learned in Haiti; we assisted at a *bois rouge* ordeal; we visited the old sorcerer of Globli who spits kola juice in the faces of little wooden mannikins; we performed our own various incantations. It was only when my cherished project of crossing over into Liberia became acute that we verged on serious disagreement. I had no special business in Liberia, but an easy march westward and a small river (the Cavally) separated us from a part of the Liberian hinterland practically inaccessible from the coast, and it seemed to me an excellent opportunity to explore it a bit, entering by this easy back door. Wamba had thrown herself into trances, sometimes suffering like an epileptic, had examined various omens—had even cut open a dog as the Greeks did their bulls and sacred doves —but every sign she could discover was negative or unfavorable. We were in a village called Golale southwest of Bin-Hounien (where Katie and I had been formerly entertained by that hospitable fratricide, San Dei). Wamba planned a final test which she declared must be conclusive. It was in our own hut, brightly lighted with one of my carbide lanterns. She placed a round-bottomed calabash bowl on a flat stone tile. Across the top of the bowl she laid a stout flat wand. One end of it pointed west toward Liberia, the other east. She called in a young man, a random villager, who had been convoked outside the hut. She stripped him completely naked, removing not only his loincloth, but even a leather bracelet and the strings in his hair. After a number of abortive efforts, she managed to get him balanced on the teetering calabash, crouched like an ape, his toes gripping the wand, preserving his balance by spreading out his arms and touching his fingers to the ground. This arranged to her satisfaction, she began to moan and sway, invoking the Fetich. Presently the calabash spun suddenly clock-wise and sent the young man sprawling, not toward Liberia, but in the opposite direction. Obviously the bowl had to spin or teeter. I am implying nothing supernormal. But Wamba was sliding into one of her abnormal states, and out of it when she stopped shuddering came her sibyl's voice, lost, far away, high-pitched:

"There is only one thing to be done. Go take a pure white cock and three white hens, carry them at night secretly across the river, set them free in Liberia, and come away. Only when they have had many progeny will it be safe for you to return there. The Fetich has spoken."

Good common sense is often hidden beneath seeming nonsense of oracular symbolism. Suppose she had said, "The Liberian hinterland is dangerous for you because there is neither any white control there nor any respect or liking for the white stranger. Wait until other whites have settled there, and then you can go in safely."

It was just this element of too intelligible prudent common sense that inclined me to assert my independence, as if it had been Katie instead of Wamba. Women were always telling you not to do something. If Wamba had said in one of her trances, "You will be killed in Liberia. The Fetich has spoken," I should not have insisted. But I think she was playing fair with her oracles. Much as she wanted to stop me, she had said a number of times, on the contrary, that I would not be killed, but that it was nevertheless a bad, bad business. All this had naturally aroused in me a vivid curiosity, partly superstitious and partly in defiance of superstition, to see just what would happen. I was tired of Wamba's bossing. I had a puppy-dog's confidence that Liberians would be nice to me, like all the other nice savages I had met.

So I told her I was going to go in spite of hell and high water, and that she could come along or not as she chose. I would take Bugler and the porters, and go as far as I liked. Mori I couldn't ask to cross the border. Not that he lacked courage, but his future lay with the French administration; it was expressly forbidden politically, and if I should chance after all to get into serious trouble, he would be badly raked over the coals for it.

The upshot was that I was to try it with Bugler and ten volunteer porters. Wamba wouldn't go against the orders of her Fetich. She was disgusted at my hard-headedness, angry and quarrelsome, but genuinely fond of me by now. She agreed to see me all the way to the river, where there was a village camp, and to await my return there. And if I was bent on engaging in this stupidity, we might as well get it over, she said. To re-assert her dominance, she insisted we set out for the border camp and sleep there so that I could start into Liberia at least fresh in broad daylight.

The trail we took that night with torches was the narrow but well-trodden main trail from Golale to the river camp, where there was a bridge of swinging vines across the Cavally. It was used mostly by Dioula peddlers, a privileged class of natives who come and go all over West

Africa unmolested. We marched uneventfully for a couple of hours and had already begun to hear the distant murmur of the river, when things went wrong. We came to a high curtain of raffia grass, hung directly across our main trail, barring it. The public trail, against all reason, had become a forbidden closed trail. I was angry and suspected trickery on Wamba's part. The presence of the barrier—evidently hung there that same afternoon—followed too pat on her warnings. But I did her an injustice. She was as surprised as the rest of us, she was playing fair with me, and far more competent to deal with obstacles of this sort. It was she, indeed, who insisted on going on. This was not trivial, for to enter a forbidden trail without sanction is to court real danger. Wamba, however, was at home in such matters. She carried her own sanctions. She was opposed to my crossing into Liberia, but the idea that any local witch-doctor business could bar her in her own forest was another matter. She had no theory of what might be occurring—probably serious, since public trails are rarely barred—but she proposed to go in immediately alone and find out. No matter what it was, she would return and take us through, she assured us. She was really splendid. She had quit her hammock as we talked. Alone she parted the grass curtain, which was lighted on our side by the torches, and disappeared into the darkness and silence beyond.

61

We waited, worried, for more than half an hour. The porters were afraid. They were saying they would not go on. Bugler said nothing, but I knew he would go anywhere. As for my own reactions, insatiable curiosity is the finest substitute for courage that I know—and the grass witch-doctor veil there, barring the trail theatrically in the dead of night, lighted fitfully by the glare of our torches, seemed a sinister dream-door to mystery. I almost wished that we might never cross its threshold, for I knew that whatever lay on the other side could never measure up to my imaginings.

When others ask what it is that drives me away from the asphalt, draws me toward deserts and jungles, I answer so sensibly with fine, fair, honest words which sound so well: love of travel, desire to see a strange thing, to learn more perhaps of savage customs, a sincere liking for primitive people—and, if I am pricked to be even more honest, the subsequent vain pleasure of seeing my name spread about in bookshops and on the tables of my friends. But all these fine fair words are empty when oneself is the ultimate questioner and no satisfying answer comes. For I have sought less consciously but just as diligently whatever it may be in places more foolishly improbable than the far places—familiar rows of street lamps in my own block, wall-paper patterns in a hotel bedroom, subway faces, want-ad pages read meaninglessly from end to end, long city streets of shop-windows peered into mechanically one by one, longer country roads, fences and tree-rows stretching, always expecting to find and never finding—I know not what. One thing is like another, and in deepest truth I do not know what drives me, or what it is I seek. I suspect sometimes that it lies not over the hill but under. I once met a man whose surprised eyes seemed to say he had found it, but he was unable to speak about it, or about anything any more.

Howbeit, the grass veil parted, and Wamba returned, blinking, out of the darkness into our torchlight. She said we could go through with her to the river camp, and from what she said I gathered that if we were to see no final thing, we were at least to see a strange one. The bridge of vines was down, was broken, fallen in the water. The river gods and demons, if propitious, would aid the mending. We could come and see what we should see, but we must follow implicitly her instructions. The porters moaned, but Wamba commanded. They moaned even more when she made them put out all the torches. We passed the barrier and went forward in darkness, though not completely dark when our eyes became accustomed, for the sky, though moonless, was bright with tropical starlight. Two men were waiting and halted us on the outskirts of the camp. They were hurried, not friendly, but acting under instructions, and respectful to

Wamba. They had a tethered goat and a big wooden
bowl. They made two porters hold the goat above the
bowl and hurriedly, like butchers, cut its throat with a
machete. Taking a cup, they hurriedly sprinkled a little
blood on our hammocks and on each piece of our baggage, seeing that no piece was overlooked, checking and
marking them with blood as customs officers do with
chalk. Wamba dipped her fingers in the bowl, smeared
a little on her own forehead, then on the foreheads of
Bugler and the porters. Then dipping both hands wrist
deep and making me lean over the bowl, she smeared
my entire face and neck, also my hands and arms, which
were bare to the elbows. She smeared also my throat
where the shirt opened, so that my white skin, I supposed,
should pass unnoticed. They took my helmet, saying they
would hide it by the trail and restore it next day. The
hammocks were left on the outskirts of the camp, but the
baggage was carried in. We entered the camp which
seemed completely deserted, piled the baggage in a hut,
and went down toward the river.

On the river's bank, beneath towering trees (to one of
which the swinging bridge of vines had been attached)
people were grouped silent, watching, waiting for something. There were several knots of them but no great
crowd. They paid no heed to us as we joined them.
Wamba held me by the hand, kept me pressed close to

her as if I was a child. There was no sound, no movement, save for occasional moans. There was only tension. It was not like anything I had ever seen except perhaps the pause before the liquefaction of the blood in the cathedral at Naples. There were no tomtoms, no wailing, no mumbo-jumbo. There was only the tension.

This tension was broken by death-bleating from darkness under the trees close by. A witch-doctor in mask and high headdress came to the water's edge, bearing a dreadful mass of entrails which glistened in the starlight. With all his strength he lifted them above his head and hurled them far out into the water. There was more tense waiting, but nothing happened. The sacrifice to the river demons was repeated. There were lighter splashes like fish jumping. Individuals were throwing bracelets and other offerings into the stream.

And then whatever it was that happened began happening.

Wamba clutched my hand tighter and pointed at the faintly rippling water's edge. At first I saw nothing. Then I saw that two ends of twisted vines were poking themselves up out of the water and crawling like living serpents, moved by no apparent human agency, up the steep bank toward the trees. They writhed like headless serpents crawling upward, dragging their long length out of the river depths, becoming thicker in body as a great emerging snake does, until they were vine cables heavy as a man's forearm.

Now the silent tension turned to shouts and action. Men seized the cables, a long line of men straining, some wading into the stream to get a hand-grip. Tugging up the slope like a road gang, they dragged out the submerged end of the fallen bridge, which they moored to a tree trunk.

Later lying in our hut, I tried to persuade Wamba to explain if she could just what had happened. Of course we got nowhere. The river demons, it seemed, had restored the bridge. If it had been salvaged by human hands only, the river demons would have ripped it down again. I asked her candidly if she didn't believe the witch-doctors had a physical hand in it. My own opinion (forced, since I have never seen any convincing proof that magic black or white can endow inanimate objects with action) was that we had witnessed a ceremony comparable to that of the Egyptian Memnon in which priestly mechanics produced the marvel. But questioning Wamba, herself an initiate priestess, was a bit like asking a Dominican mother superior whether roses had really fallen from the sky at Lima. So I went to sleep in Wamba's arms, content that I had seen a strange sight, but wishing that I could believe I had seen a miracle.

Next morning, leaving my sorceress, who promised to wait faithfully at the river camp but who exhausted her Bambara to express how great a fool she thought me, we crossed over into Liberia.

IV

No MAGIC of Wamba's and no merit of mine—
but only the accident of an old pair of boots,
and another man's boots at that, though I
happened to be wearing them—got me and my porters
with whole skins and baggage out of Liberia eventually.

Of course we had no business to be going in by this
back door—not even if Wamba's oracles had been favorable. Liberia down on the seacoast is a different matter.
American Negroes, descendants of freed slaves, administer a black republic which goes not too badly on its
ocean fringes. But the extreme Liberian hinterland has
a bad name.

If I had possessed proper objective, equipment, and
authority, things might have gone differently, but I was
wandering off on a wild excursion with no better motives
than curiosity and a wish to get loose for a while from
Wamba's apron-strings, with no personnel except Bugler
and a dozen scared but loyal porters. It hardly required
sibylline prophecy or the ripped-out insides of unhappy

68

dogs and chickens to foretell that we should very likely get into trouble of some sort.

Yet except for the novelty of traversing the Cavally River on a swaying vine bridge constructed by demons and fit only for apes, our crossing from Ivory Coast territory into Liberia was at first impression an unconvincing displacement, like going from France into Belgium or from Cincinnati to Detroit. One says, "Well, here I am in a different place," but the saying it doesn't mean much since everything is just the same.

The forest was identical, the trails likewise, and the few people we met seemed in no way different from our own amiable Yafouba savages. But this was only for the first few miles. As we went deeper in, we began to sense vaguely and then more definitely that this was not a friendly place. Nor was this a trick played by imagination, conjured up by Wamba's warnings and forebodings. All wayfaring natives go armed, of course, in the great forest. But such Ivory Coast wayfarers as we had been accustomed to encounter would always stand in the trail, greet us and joke with us, ask questions as we passed. An assegai or a bow with poisoned arrows is a delightful touch of local color in the hands of a black naked forest man who stands gay and grinning. But it loses most of its charm when the man darts silently into the bush fifty yards ahead of you and lurks invisible behind the leaves until you have passed by. The natives here were stealthy and unfriendly. I didn't like it, and my porters didn't like it at all. Bugler was too proud to show whether he liked it or not. He marched straight ahead superbly, and we followed. As a matter of fact it was a bad place where frequently the casual passing stranger, even the at-home Liberian going from village to village, was stalked and taken like other game; where even the Dioula peddlers went only by day, in armed companies. It was, by the way, the only territory of this sort which I ever touched in my somewhat wide wanderings over West Africa.

We were heading southwest toward a village called Zanbli where there was supposed to be a small Liberian government post with a sort of administrator in charge. Our intention was to spend the night there, get what help and information the administrator could give us, and go deeper in, if all went well, on the following day. We hurried along, a bit nervous and jumpy, anxious to make Zanbli before sundown. I felt sure that once in contact with an administration post, however isolated in the bush, we would be well received, for America and Liberia are notoriously friendly. Quite likely, they might lend us guides and guards for our further excursioning.

Actually nothing whatever happened to us on the trail to Zanbli. Never once were we menaced or halted. On the contrary we were avoided. We traversed hut clusters, seemingly deserted, without seeing a human face. The fine mess that awaited us had no saving cinema qualities. It was, in fact, disgustingly undramatic.

We reached Zanbli about four o'clock in the afternoon —some twenty mud-thatched huts scattered outside a central stockade which was evidently the administration post, for a dirty little flag surmounted it. A few villagers stared at us from a distance, but none came near us even to offer the customary water. The stockade gate was ajar. I parked my porters, hammock, and baggage in front of it, with Bugler in charge, and went inside alone. A Liberian corporal, barefooted and trouserless, but wearing a shabby scarlet soldier's coat and with a proper rifle, halted me and asked in pidjin what I wanted. Three or four other soldiers, similarly garbed and armed, lolled about. There was a big square mud house, windowed, with a veranda, evidently a sort of office, from which the flag flew; also a dwelling, but no sign of life in either. I said I was an American traveler and wanted to see the administrator. "Mister Harris," said the guard, as one would say it in plain homely American. It was a comfort to hear him say "Mister Harris." Now everything would be all right. Very likely it would turn out that Mr. Harris and I had mutual acquaintances in Harlem or Tuskegee. At any rate we could talk of Booker Washington. I mounted the office veranda, asked the guard for a drink of water, and lighted a cigarette as if I owned the place. I already felt welcome, and perhaps just a little patronizing. America was a lot bigger than Liberia, and I had read somewhere that they had copied their Constitution from ours. I thought of the interesting conversation we might also have about Haiti. I sat waiting for a quarter of an hour or so, thinking smugly how well things always turned out for me, and the delay seemed all right too, since Mr. Harris had probably been interrupted in his siesta.

Presently Mr. Harris emerged from his house, and I arose to meet him. His appearance was as comforting as his homely name. He was a middle-aged dark Negro in horn-rimmed spectacles, store-bought stiff straw hat, civilian khaki, celluloid collar, and stringy black necktie. He might have just come out of the drugstore at the corner of Seventh Avenue and One Hundred and Thirty-sixth Street. He looked like a school-teacher type, probably bored by his isolation here, and hospitable. It was only after his soft, boneless handshake that I realized the eyes behind the spectacles were not so reassuring. Not that they were savage or hostile. But they were the shifty, uncandid eyes of a man who has got something up his sleeve and is not at ease. Also I realized that he hadn't yet spoken. I had addressed him in polite colloquial American English, sure that he would respond with the same. But now when he opened his mouth, it was clear that he knew scarcely any English. It was gross pidjin he talked, and Bambara. I was beginning to be a little impatient and resentful, with a faint edge of aggressiveness in my resentment. For he hadn't even asked me to sit down, nor made any commonest offer of refreshment. I sat down without being asked and said in his own gross but adequate medium, measuring my words:

"Look here, I am not either a trader or a political, wanting any profit from you. I am a private American traveler, a writer of books. Everywhere in French Africa I have been well received by blacks and whites. Now I am in your country, which as you must surely know is friendly with America. Furthermore I have brought all my own food and supplies. I would like to stay a few days if you can put me up tonight in your village guesthouse. If your tribal chiefs care to visit me, there will be generous gifts for them, and I would like in turn to visit some of their villages. What about it, Mr. Harris?"

To which Mr. Harris replied in a queer, aggressive, but embarrassed tone, "Show me your papers."

"What's the matter with you?" I said. "My passport is out there in my tin trunk somewhere, and if you insist I'll go and get it."

"No," he interrupted, "I mean your papers from Monrovia, your papers from the Liberian government."

I said, "But you know perfectly well that I have come down from the north, not up from the coast, and could have no papers from your capital or your government. You know that you are the first Liberian official of any sort I've met."

"So you have no Liberian papers," he said, and while he said it in a blaming tone, I knew that for some reason not yet disclosed he was glad I had no Liberian papers, and was wanting to make sure. There was something sour, and it was getting more sour every minute. I stood up.

I said, "Well, here I am. What are you going to do about it? You are the local authority, and if you don't want me in your territory, tell me to get out, and I'll go back where I came from."

And right there the cat poked a clawed paw out of the bag where it had been hiding. "You have invaded our territory," said Mr. Harris; "it is grave." I said, "It is pure God-damned nonsense and you know it. What are you up to anyway? You are an official. You can't get away with anything like that."

But I was far from sure just what he might get away with. Any communication with Monrovia would take more than a month. He was saying, "I ask you, please, to wait." I was caught, and somewhat ignominiously. It wasn't the four armed guards who had stopped lolling and were on the job. I could have walked out of the stockade, or at least I believed I could. But it was within an hour of sundown, and we wouldn't have had a gambling chance to get out of Mr. Harris's territory. He went away and I waited, lighting another cigarette. I was more annoyed and angry than seriously worried, but it wasn't pleasant. Almost immediately he returned with an elderly Kroumen (a forest tribe man), robed, goat-bearded, hookish-nosed, with a face that was more savagely evil than his own, but less evasive and decidedly more intelligent. He spoke doubtful pidjin. He was evidently not officially connected with the post. He was Mr. Harris's personal familiar and adviser. Mr. Harris wanted me to repeat all I had previously said. But if Mr. Harris needed reinforcements, I needed them even more. I wished fervently for Mori. I could only send one of the guards for Bugler, saying I would need him to interpret. He came proudly in his tattered coat and wig of monkey fur, bugle at ease in his left hand, saluting so smartly that the guards snapped to attention. When Bugler walked like that, it was a military parade. He stood gravely beside my chair. The Kroumen looked at him intently and asked him a question which sounded insulting, in a language which I had never heard. Bugler's face went blank and he replied in Bambara, *"Ti famou"* ("I don't understand"). The Kroumen tried again. Bugler's face went blanker still, apologetic. So that was that. We did the best we could in pidjin. But presently the Kroumen and Mr. Harris, with a narrow eye at first on Bugler, began holding side conferences in their own language. . . .

That night, after they had put us in a guarded hut, abandoning even the pretense that we were anything but prisoners, Bugler gave me a graphic and complete, though whispered, version of the conference thus eavesdropped, and which had ended inconclusively, something like this:

Mr. Harris: "You saw all that baggage out there. He told us he has food and a lot of gifts. He probably has a lot of rum too, and ammunition. And you saw that shotgun."

The Kroumen: "I tell you to look at his trousers there. I don't like his trousers either. And I tell you to look again at his boots."

Mr. Harris: "But he told us himself he was just a private traveler. Besides, look at the way he carries himself. Part of the time he was polite and afraid of us. You could see it. He carries no way of commanding."

The Kroumen: "It is not his face or his way, I tell you. It is his clothes. I have been on boats that came from England. His clothes are dirty, but I don't like them. And the boots are hateful. They are the boots of a white man who commands. I have looked for sewing on his coat-sleeves and it is true that there are no marks. But you will find his gold stripes put away somewhere in his trunk, and you will be sorry. It is not safe to do it. There will be trouble afterward."

So that was what it was all about. With the best good will in the world, they wanted to rob us, but they couldn't quite make up their minds that it would be safe. It was so simple that, except for the doubtful taste of doing it under cover of Mr. Harris's officialdom, one could understand if not entirely sympathize with them in their embarrassing predicament. Yet even academically as well as personally, I disliked this Mr. Harris. For, according to Bugler's further revelations, it was not the keen-faced savage Kroumen, but the on the whole rather dull, soft-handed, thick-faced Mr. Harris who had finally suggested a less pleasant method of solving the problem. He had suggested, in brief, that if it seemed unsafe to confiscate our belongings and let us go free to make trouble afterward, it might be possible to send us away at an hour when night would forcedly overtake us, and arrange to have the whole matter concluded as quietly as possible on the trail. But this suggestion the Kroumen had also opposed violently, and Bugler, who had smelled real trouble on the veranda, was of the opinion now that there was less cause for worry. He strongly advised against making a break. We risked no harm in the hut there. And when

77

morning came we would see, forewarned, what could be done. I thought his advice was sensible and tried to go to sleep.

But it occurred to me as I lay there that this somewhat dull Mr. Harris, with his school-teacher air, his Fourteenth Street stiff straw hat, horn-rimmed spectacles, and little stringy black necktie askew in a celluloid collar, was perhaps the only really dangerous Negro I had ever encountered in the African jungle.

The old Kroumen was a savage, and if a man's physiognomy and eyes ever mean anything, he was the more ruthless, perhaps even the more rapacious, of the two. But he was not stupid. It was his deterrent imagination, stimulated by the hazard of the boots, that saved us from the dull Mr. Harris. Those boots, in fact, had never been made for mine or any civilian feet. They had been made by the best military bootmaker in London, and were of the sort worn by generals, colonels, and occasionally majors with millionaire aunts or wives. They had been ordered by my friend Major Russell Haven Davis in 1925, in Haiti—and they had pinched his feet. So he had swapped them to me for a tennis racket and a German camera. Now after five years, though badly down at heel, they still retained a vestige of their martial glory which the Kroumen had sensed and found not to his liking.

Therefore, next morning, since this Kroumen proved to be the dominant rascal of the two, Mr. Harris came, announcing that we were free to return whence we had come, and added that his only reason for advising us strongly neither to linger nor to go farther was that the territory was not safe for strangers. On this point, I found myself quite heartily, and for the first time, in accord with Mr. Harris. Two of my porters had skipped during the night, but the others gathered and we prepared to go. Mr. Harris had the dull impudence to hang round with a sick crocodilish smile, watching us distribute the loads and offering advice. The Kroumen I never saw again. He was made of different stuff. He was through. Presently a woman brought eggs and a chicken, nodding to Mr. Harris. I said to her, ignoring him, "Bring also the villager who supplied them, that I may pay him." Mr. Harris said, "No, they are a gift." I said, "No, thank you, I am not accepting any gifts in Liberia, and neither am I giving any." We were hurrying and ready to leave. Mr. Harris drew Bugler aside. "He is hoping," said Bugler, "that you will give him at least a bottle of rum and some tins of sardines." I was fed up. I said, "I'll be damned if I will. I will give all the rum I've got to you and my friends across the river."

This restored a little of my self-respect, but not much. It was an unprideful going away. That we went with a

79

whole shirt was due neither to ruse nor to valor that could be bragged of later. I had lost face with myself, and had lost face a little with my porters. They knew I had been licked, and that we had narrowly escaped worse, negatively.

Recrossing the Cavally—to a place where everybody was friendly and people waited who were fond of me—would be a comfort of getting home, but Wamba would know how to take most of the joy out of that with her well-justified I-told-you-so's. I had run away from Wamba, and I was coming back with my tail between my legs.

She was waiting at the river camp, where anxious Mori had rejoined her with the rest of my porters. They came down to the bank and shouted questions as we recrossed the vine bridge, for we had hoped to be gone perhaps a week. We had a sheep killed, and while it was cooking, Bugler and I told our story. When we came to the part about the boots, Wamba made me repeat it and stopped her scolding. It seemed to mean something to her that it hadn't meant to me. Her way of understanding it was a way quite different from my white way of understanding. If I could reproduce in white language her black conception of the episode's significance, it would throw some light, I think, on real Fetichist psychology. But it is going to be difficult, and if I can do it at all, it will be by comparison with certain of our more familiar white conceptions.

Forcedly I regarded the episode of the boots as simply a lucky accident. Wamba, on the other hand, believes that nothing is an accident. She believed, therefore, in this case, that the whole Liberian incident was written implicitly and fore-ordained in my acquiring of the boots five years previously. She believed that in acquiring them, I unconsciously obeyed the voice of a Fetich (here something like our old conception of a guardian angel) and that the boots themselves were consequently *grigris;* that they contained and controlled this future fate in embryo. For just as the Harlem Negro believes that the clearing-house lottery numbers tomorrow may be "dreamed" in advance, and therefore must exist already somewhere in the embryonic future, Wamba believes that all possible future events exist in embryo. This sounds like purest fatalism, but it is not. For she believes also that the future, if foreseen, may be to some degree controlled. And the real purpose of Fetich consultation and divination is to decipher and control the future. Those of us whites who are fatalists at all usually believe in a predestination, or providence, or kismet, which cannot be changed or escaped from. What is going to be, will be, we say. But Wamba believes differently. She believes that fate, though written, projects itself into the future not as a straight line, but *fan-shaped*, in myriad alternate paths multiplying to infinity. She conveyed this difficult concept of fan-shaped destiny by an ingenious analogy:

I am walking in an unknown forest. There are as many directions to walk as there are points of the compass. I know nothing of what awaits me in any direction, but in all directions fate awaits me, things already written in the sense that they exist already, and are there inevitable, but alternate, depending on the path I take. In one path there is a tree from which I will pluck refreshing fruit. In another, a panther waits to leap upon me. Beside another path, there is a good spring of water. In another direction, there is an elephant trap into which I will fall and be impaled on the stakes. In still another, a friendly camp where I will be well treated. All these things are written fan-shaped in the future. And all are true potentials. And we must assume, as so often is the case in the actual forest of human life, that no process of logic or reason can disclose whether it is better for me to turn to right or left. And since I am continually moving in some path or other from the womb to the grave, since even stopping to stand still is a form of moving, no tiniest choice in the most trivial matter, no event, itself however trivial, is without its potentiality to change one's future life.

Therefore the Negro primitive consults the Fetich;

therefore he devises charms and *grigris* to protect him in the labyrinth. If we have no faith in his methods, we can at least begin to understand why he deems it necessary to try to do something. We whites often recognize, and sometimes with a shock, that despite all our processes of logical foresight, we also walk in this blind labyrinth, not knowing where any path will lead. But our very logic seems to teach us that there is nothing we can do about it. The gate clangs shut and you miss your train by a split second because you fumbled for change when you bought a morning newspaper; and in the evening newspaper you read the list of the dead. Usually the drama is less sudden, less spectacular, less final, but if you look back you will discover just as fatally a hundred cases in which seemingly pointless hazards or decisions changed your life. Will you come over and make a fourth at bridge this evening? No, I've got some work to do. . . . You are hesitating and your friend has almost hung up the telephone receiver. Just before it clicks, you say, "Oh, well, I'll come over anyway." During the evening a girl drops in whom you have never seen nor heard of, and six months afterward you find yourself married to her. Fate, providence, blind luck, or Wamba's fan-shaped future. A pair of boots in Haiti pinched Major Davis's feet. That was five years ago. Tomorrow, for all I know, I may do some pointless thing like going to the corner café for a pack of cigarettes, and set in train another absurd sequence that will make me five years hence a multimillionaire or put me in the gutter.

Now the basic difference between Wamba's mind and mine, or yours, is that while we regard all such sequences as unpredictable and therefore uncontrollable, she believes they form a mysterious pattern and can be to some degree deciphered. This, I think, is one of the fundamental elements of the black primitive psychology. In the fan-shaped labyrinth of life where neither logic nor consciously directed will seems adequate, the Negro seeks for supernormal guidance in his Fetiches, somewhat as the old-time Christian sought it on his knees in prayer. Most of us who are more enlightened cross our fingers or flip a coin.

V

IN THE early course of Ivory Coast wanderings, after my misadventure in Liberia, we visited an old witch-doctor who, Wamba said, was very powerful in divination.

He was an unpretentious graybeard who received us on a mat before his hut, surrounded by no blatant or horrific mumbo-jumbo. He sat staring for a while at nothing visible, and then began to speak of forest birds. He spoke presently of the toucan, which is a large bird, of brilliant flame-jeweled plumage, with a weird, far cry. It rests on highest tree-tops, is very difficult to approach, and flies usually toward the evening.

He said: "The toucan calls there close by, and you follow. He flies farther, and you follow. You go on and on. You see his bright plumage, but then he is gone. You came here following a bright toucan. It flies before you, and where it flies you follow."

I said, "Yes, old wise black man, but tell me, please, will I ever catch the toucan?"

85

"Eh, that who knows?" he said. "But you will always follow."

So we went away toward the evening, as the toucan flies, but following what bright bird I know not. We were planning to arrive back, circling, ten days later, in the ancestral village of the chief San Dei, where we had been invited to participate in sacrifices that would be offered on the tomb of his brother Bou. But meanwhile we were wandering wide and free. And if we caught no flamed chimera, we had at least some curious experiences which only the presence and friendship of an amiable witch like Wamba could have made possible for a roving white. Without her, indeed, one would have been hospitably received, but completely excluded from the special things, unaware even that they were occurring.

We arrived one afternoon in the central village of a chief called Mabya, asking shelter for the night. This Mabya had panther teeth braided in his hair and seemed on first impression a formidable personage. Our welcome, though hospital enough, was not exuberant. His *griot* was a rather savage fellow who seemed to be in a permanent bad humor, and not partial to traveling strangers. When we met the chief for the usual preliminary palaver, the *griot* glared about as if daring any one to contradict him, and shouted, "When his father made him, he made a panther."

We agreed politely that this was true, but the *griot*
seemed unmollified. He continued:

> *At present it is time to talk,*
> *But no one dares to talk roughly with him.*
> *This is the great forest*
> *Where all men must walk gently.*
> *This is the great forest;*
> *Only the panther is at home here.*

The Panther himself proved to be, however, on closer
contact, a very benevolent and good-natured panther. In
addition to the profusion of teeth braided in his hair,
he wore a felt hat cocked on one side, and had a sympathetic face in which it seemed to me there was a certain
wily humor. One gathered that the *griot's* words were
merely a manner of speaking. Panther Teeth saw us
comfortably installed in the guest-house and offered what
immediate hospitality of palm wine, meats, and fruit the
village afforded. Even the shouting *griot* turned out to
be in private life an amiable soul and brought us six
fresh eggs that evening.

Before we settled down to feel at home, however, in
this village, I had a serious quarrel, but it developed
quite on the side, and from a wholly different quarter.
It developed late on that same night. I had already gone
to sleep when Mori came with the porters' headman, say-

ing that the porters had not eaten. There were about twenty porters with me, including some of the original ones from Dananae. Out of their own pay, which was the equivalent of six cents a day, they provided their own food for morning and noon, a bit of cold cooked rice or manioc. Sometimes they elected to go the whole day without eating, which was their own affair, since they were well paid and could get what they needed for the value of less than a penny. But at night they always had to be supplied with a belly-bursting meal—and for this the cost and responsibility rested wholly on me.

The price of this meal, its nature, its cost, and the manner of providing it, are fairly standardized. As soon as you enter a village, planning to spend the night, you arrange with this or that private family, which either volunteers or is designated by the local chief, to feed your porters. You pay the man of the family in advance the equivalent of two cents per head, which is the accepted price, fair and adequate. For this he provides great bowls of rice and smaller bowls of hot sauce which must contain okra or some other vegetable, salt, and red pepper, with meat or fish scrapped through the sauce to give it body and flavor. The man's wives and family usually prepare this, which takes time, but gives them a good profit.

In this village I had made the usual arrangement, and

now, supposing there had simply been a longer delay than usual, sent Mori to see about it. He returned after a little while and came inside the hut.

"It is true that the porters have not eaten," he said, "and there is something not right. I found the man, but he was not in his own compound, and avoided me. He told me it was because the sauce his wives had made was not good, and that he was ashamed to give it to the porters, and that they were preparing more. But when I asked him to show me the cooked rice then, he could not show me any, and I do not believe he has cooked any. I believe that he does not mean to feed them."

I lighted my carbide lantern, pulled on my boots, and went with him in pajamas down into the village, which was dark. My porters were holding the man. They were gathered in front of his dark compound, and though usually patient and humble, they would not let him go until I had seen him.

He first repeated what he had said to Mori. "The sauce was not good and I am already making other." I said, "Where then is the cooked rice, and where are the fires?" He said, "In my sister's compound, not here in the village." Then seeing me getting angry and not believing him, he said, "Alas, my cousin to whom I entrusted the money—"

I smashed him on the head with my cocomacaque stick,

and when he fell not completely stunned, crawling and trying to take hold of my feet and whining, I smashed him again and began kicking him with my boots to do him an injury as he lay on the ground. Mori made me stop, and I was glad that he made me stop, but I was glad also for what I had done.

We aroused the man's family and made them light fires, and Mori remained to see that the porters were fed.

Next morning the chief sent for me and I went, wondering if there would perhaps be trouble. But he had already investigated the matter to his satisfaction. He said that as soon as the man recovered he would have him badly beaten again in the presence of his wives and of the village. He said that the village was pleased and that they all hoped we would prolong our visit. For this invitation, however, it developed, he had a special reason which did not concern me so directly. They had learned who Wamba was, and it seemed that in Panther-Teeth's river-camp village not far distant, there was a little affair that she might be just the person to help straighten out. It would be a great service to Panther-Teeth if she could get to the bottom of it, he said, because he was very fond of fresh fish and hadn't had any for a number of weeks. To be precise, his fisherman had been bewitched and the fish would no longer enter the wicker basket traps, though, as everybody knew, the river was still full of them. And up to now his local Fetichers hadn't been able to do anything.

So Wamba went to the other village on that same day to investigate, refusing to let me go with her for fear that my presence would hamper her activities. Panther-Teeth, pleased at her promise to help him, sent for his drummers and dancers to entertain us meanwhile, and in the afternoon great quantities of banghi flowed. The *griot* was there, no longer glaring, and deigned to make a little song about me as "the one who dealt heavy blows justly." I produced the usual gifts, including a striped Dioula robe and a clasp-knife for Panther-Teeth, also a briquet, the dry-mesh sort, with which he was delighted. But he didn't care for my Amer Picon. (I had opened a bottle, thinking to offer him a special treat). He spat it out on the ground, eyeing me as if I had played a bad joke on him. He said it tasted like medicament.

Here for the first time a man came with a carved figure which he offered to sell me. It was old and rather good. I had been wary about asking to buy masks or carvings, for the good ones are usually religious or ancestral. And besides, I had no wish to be treated as a trader. But since the offer now came spontaneously, I was glad to benefit. So I bought the figure at the man's own price, and asked Panther-Teeth to have it announced that if there were any who had masks, statuettes, or bracelets which they cared to sell willingly, I would buy without disputing. He sent men rounding up what could be found, and presently there was a good-sized pile of it—no marvelous museum pieces, but good Ivory Coast stuff which one almost never sees now in territory touched by motors. I left the fixing of prices entirely to them and to Panther-Teeth, saying that each owner must make me the price which he and they all deemed proper among themselves. There was a lot of chattering in which I took no part. The prices they finally agreed on as just were values ranging from the equivalent of twenty to thirty cents for a mask or carved figure and ten to fifteen cents for a massive brass bracelet, often beautifully carved. Not to be generous or patronizing, but to preserve some shred of a feeling of my own decency, if ever so little, I compromised on paying the double asked for each. Most of them were objects worth easily from twenty-five to fifty dollars in Europe, even more in New York. People talk and write of being cheated by rapacious natives, and so you certainly are if you don't watch your step in big markets and towns on the highways. But in the bush the opposite is often embarrassingly true.

Two brothers of Panther-Teeth had appeared early in the afternoon, one in a squirrel-skin cap with tails attached, like Daniel Boone, the other in a derby. They were minor chiefs and sat beside us. They had brought

me a very big bowl of raw rice, piled high, on which
reposed a monstrous dead dried catfish, black and hard
as wood, curled round himself, with his tail in his mouth.
He looked as royal as a papier-mâché peacock in a festal
Max Reinhardt banquet procession, but I knew that he
was full of little bones and would outstink a nest of
minks when he began cooking. So I gave him surreptitiously to Mori, who put him away in his baggage and
who still had him when we returned to Dananae weeks
later. From time to time Panther-Teeth and I had been
retiring to my hut, as if to a speakeasy, for a drop of
rum. After the two brothers came, it was polite to invite
them also.

The dances, mask-buyings, gift-givings, were now over.
We notables sat in the public square while the assembled
villagers, men, women, babies, dogs, and goats, stood or
squatted around in a solid circle, watching us sit. I must
explain that sitting is a frequent pastime for notables in
the forest. Life isn't all excitement and beating on tomtoms. You just sit, several of you, not even gossiping,
not waiting for anything, like an old woman and her
shadows in a rocking-chair on a farm veranda in Kansas.
Except that usually several hundred people watch you
sit, as if you were the Prince of Wales. When one writes
of adventure, there is a tendency to gloss the parts that
were not adventurous. But looking back, it seems to me

that a full third of the time I have spent intimately among primitive groups, whether in jungle, mountain, or desert, has been spent in sitting. Normally this time we would have just sat until dark, or until we got hungry.

Toward five o'clock, however, Panther-Teeth bestirred himself, contrary to all local social precedent. He announced that he and Mori and I were going for a little stroll. The two brothers deemed this an agreeable idea and prepared to accompany us. Panther-Teeth explained again that it was he and I and Mori who were going for the stroll. So we started, and when we got to the outskirts of the village, we found not only the two brothers at our heels but the entire population following us. Panther-Teeth demanded loudly to know whether he was the big chief or whether he wasn't. They stood crestfallen, sadly watching our departure.

All this struck me as a slightly mysterious if trivial performance. Ivory Coast chiefs do not habitually invite their guests for casual strolls. "What do you suppose he is up to?" I asked Mori in French as we disappeared from sight of the village, along a little side trail. Mori replied that he hadn't any idea.

It was a one-man trail, and we padded along single file, with Panther-Teeth in the lead. Very soon we came to a trail barrier, but not a Fetich barrier—merely a sign of private domain. Then on we went, saying nothing and seeing nothing for fully three kilometers. Mori and I finally began to get hot and tired and to complain. Why hadn't we taken hammocks and porters if we were going so far, and was this a joke, or what was it all about anyway?

Panther-Teeth, smiling like a baby, said, "No, it's just a little way farther. I want to show you my ducks. . . ."

"Is he making fun of us?" I asked Mori.

"No," said Mori, "he's got something to show us, and we must humor him."

So we went on for another kilometer and arrived ridiculously in the heart of the jungle at a prosperous duck farm. Why it seemed to me so ridiculously incredible there, like a railroad buffet restaurant or an ice factory, I don't know, unless because it was so completely commonplace. It surprised me more than if it had been the mythical white goddess. Five thousand miles into the heart of the black African jungle, with the last long miles on foot, led by a savage chief with panther teeth braided in his hair—to see a duck farm.

A proper poultry yard—it was just that. True, it was surrounded by bamboo instead of chicken-wire, and the caretakers' houses were mud-thatched, but when you looked at the dozens of ducks waddling about and quacking, dozens of little ducklings too, and Panther-Teeth clucked to them, and they came waddling around you, and he gave you handfuls of corn to feed them, and asked you to see how fat they were—you were out of Africa and back on Hal Smith's farm in Connecticut, and after you had fed and praised the ducks and said how cunning the ducklings were, and then there wasn't anything much else to do about it, you'd go back up to the house and mix cocktails and turn on the phonograph.

We sat for a while and tossed the corn and praised the ducks and said how cunning the ducklings were, and then there didn't seem to be anything much else to do about it, and it was coming twilight; so we started back to the house.

We dropped behind a little on the trail, and I said, "Now, Mori, you have seen it, will you please tell me what it was all about—why he brought us there?"

Mori said, "Well, I have been thinking, and I think I know. The chief here couldn't send his two brothers away, for they were guests. With us remaining, they also would have remained, and wherever we went in the village they would have politely accompanied us. But when we get back it will be after dark, and they will be gone. You will see."

I offer this analytical gem of Mori's to the learned Dr. Lévy-Brühl for his next Sorbonne volume on the soul

and mentality of the primitive. I have a great respect for
Dr. Lévy-Brühl, and he is welcome to it. There is certainly nothing I can do about it. For Mori was right.
We had walked ten miles to look at some God-damned
ducks in order that Panther-Teeth might guzzle my
bottle of rum without sharing it with his brothers.

When Bugler came with coffee next morning, Wamba
was asleep on the mat beside me. She had returned from
the river village late in the night, tired, and hadn't
bothered to awaken me. However, she was full of news.
All that Panther-Teeth had cared about, apparently, was
getting his fresh fish, but the bewitchment of the fisherman, who was a popular young fellow, involved more
than his wicker traps, and the river village was in an
angry turmoil. It was a double bewitchment that had
come upon the fisherman. His wicker basket fish-traps no
longer caught fish. But also he was unable to stand up
and go in to his wife. And it was this, even more than
the other, that distressed him and outraged the small community. All primitive peoples, of course, regard the erect
phallus both in symbol and in flesh as the mainspring of
all things, the only link between yesterday and tomorrow,
the only bridge between chaos and eternity. They recognize both mystically and at the same time in its purest
physical simplicity the obvious truth which our church

spires, Easter lilies, newborn babes, and obelisks attest, but which with our different sense of propriety we face perhaps less frankly.

So that when Wamba had arrived, she told me, the entire village had taken this most important of all matters publicly in charge. There was to be a trial by ordeal —no rare occurrence, but the commonest method of solving such problems of guilt in the forest when ordinary divination failed. As for herself, she was simply to be one of the umpires, a natural choice, since she was a person of known magical prestige, yet completely outside personal motivations touching the village group, and therefore agreeable to all factions. It was to be completely public. She had to go back that morning. Did I want to come along with her now, or follow later? I could see it, then? But anybody could. That's what she was telling me. . . .

So we went down to the river village, and thanks entirely to Wamba rather than to any foreknowledge or initiative of my own, we saw the whole proceedings.

In my opinion (after having met and talked with the young fisherman—his name was Koro—and after having had a look at him and his fish-traps) we had before us here a case of authentic, actual bewitchment, that is to say, black sorcery in effectual operation, whatever you may choose to suppose black sorcery to be. Its elements had a quality of sharp definiteness which did not pass the limits of what I knew that evilly directed sorcery could do. His double misfortune, his double impotence, had come upon him about two weeks before. And there was no reason for either of these misfortunes, that is, really, no normal ordinary reason. This we were invited, even urged, to verify. We went to the river and inspected the fish-traps. He was an expert fisherman. And the river was still full of fish. With equal simplicity, he stripped off his breech-clout to show himself strongly and manfully made. He was a healthy young male animal. He had a young desirable wife who was also presented for our inspection. Prior to the misfortune, he had caught all the fish he wanted, and had known his wife as much as he wanted. All the mechanics and all the opportunity were still there unchanged. But suddenly Koro could no longer catch any fish, and he could no longer stand up and go in to his wife. The whole village believed that he was bewitched, and I believed it too. I mean that I believed it literally, without shifty materialistic-rational qualification of any sort. Real magic is never materialistic. And here were precisely the things which I know witchcraft can do. Please understand the sharp limitation of my assertion. I do not believe that witchcraft can crack a skull or make a wall fall down. But witchcraft can destroy a man and can destroy a house by means more subtle though just as deadly.

Concerning the means they planned to use for the discovery of the guilty person, I felt less certainty of magical conviction. For when any group is put under a prolonged and dangerous nervous strain, the guilty individual is quite likely to be the one who cracks. But Wamba, who should know a great deal more about it than I do, said my reasoning was beside the point, that the Fetich really worked in the poison, and that to prove it she—or I, if I chose—being totally innocent and outside the affair, could drink a gallon of the stuff, whereas, as I should see, the guilty one would be writhing in agony.

Be that as it may, if the proceedings which followed were typical, they went to prove at least one thing—that an extraordinary amount of nonsense has been written about forest poison ordeals, particularly about their crooked faked control by the witch-doctors.

The poison had been brought in from the forest that morning, a bushel at least of thick, freshly cut bark from a tree called the Yri-ble (red tree or blood tree). The whole village was gathered round, watching the preparations for brewing it into a liquid. I picked up and examined some pieces. They were big rough chunks, six or eight inches in diameter, about two inches thick. The outside was black, rough, corrugated, like an elephant's skin. The inside, where it had peeled off from the wood, was an ugly, rich, fat fibrous substance, with streaks of red serrated with white fat streaks. The red streaks were slightly granulated like drying blood. It glistened wetly and exuded thick drops. It was more like animal tissue than vegetable. It was like colored pictures of tissue in anatomy books.

The brewing was not a ritual or witch-doctor business at all. What surprised me was that it was as matter-of-fact as mixing a big bowl of punch—except for the keen-eyed watching of the three umpires, who were the fisherman's father, the local witch-doctor, and Wamba—except also for the keen-eyed close unofficial watching of the eighteen or twenty persons who must undergo the ordeal. These the commands of the Fetich had gradually weeded out from the small community. The point here is difficult to explain. For they were not all suspect in our police-court sense. They were selected only, as nearly as Wamba could make me understand, "as being the ones capable of having done it." Curiously enough, Fisherman himself, as accuser, must also drink, as must the three umpires.

A big iron family cook-pot, the largest in the village, had been brought, scrubbed with sand, and filled with water. Holding a chunk of bark over the pot, a man began scraping with a dull iron knife. As the scrapings dropped into the water, a woman stirred with a stick. The effect on the surface of the water was exactly as if they were adding soap. It lathered and foamed pure white on top, but the water underneath became gradually an opaque dirty red. The man scraped at least a dozen chunks into the water, while the three umpires tasted from time to time, spitting it out afterward. Finally they agreed it had the proper strength.

Although it was late in the afternoon, the sun was still hot and there was a discussion as to where the drinking should take place—stupidly, I thought, like people arguing about where they should spread a picnic. They decided on a stony platform, shaded, at the river's edge. Thither the bowl was carried, sloshing. The witch-doctor, who had meanwhile put on his headdress, came masked and ringing a bell and made mumbo-jumbo over it, calling on the Fetich to deal justice. It was like opening a murder trial with prayer. For the first time it began to seem serious and real—a little shuddery if you like. The casualness up to then had prevented me from feeling any sense of reality, almost disappointed me that it had not been more theatrical.

What followed also, for a time at least, was matter-of-fact rather than dramatic. The eighteen, whom I now counted, ten women and eight men, of various ages, all stripped of their personal *grigris* to prevent counter-magic, sat in a loose circle with the pot in the middle. Around the pot were the three umpires, including Wamba, the accusing fisherman, and myself, permitted to sit there as Wamba's protégé.

There was a calabash cup, gourd-handled, also scraped with sand, about the size of an ordinary goblet. The witch-doctor first filled and drained it in a single draught, then the umpire who was Fisherman's father, then Wamba, then Fisherman himself. Then, one at a time, each of the eighteen arose and came and drank, returning to sit in the circle. The big bowl was still three-fourths full, and I wondered why so much had been brewed. Wamba said it was because one never knew how much would be needed, that they would presently drink again, and keep on drinking until something manifested itself. Meanwhile they sat quietly, with strained, waiting faces.

I felt myself getting vaguely uncomfortable, beginning to be nervous—and then unpleasantly realized why. The thing inside me which makes me sometimes do things against all rhyme or reason was stirring and poking at me. It was an urgency not at all of courage and not exactly of curiosity, but the old, almost stupid urge, the psychological or pathological necessity to taste and experience everything possible. (Perhaps also, no matter how silly it may sound, there was a slight embarrassment akin to social self-consciousness, due to the fact that all the others were participating and I alone was left out.) But this is all probably too finely spun to be the truth. It simply came upon me that I had to drink some of the stuff, as a child will deliberately hurt itself, or as Chekov's man found it necessary to let a dog bite him. This last is the nearest, if you can understand it.

I said, "Wamba, don't you think I ought to drink some of it too?" She was not surprised, and not worried. She said, "You are a black white man, not like another. You can do as you please about it. You didn't bewitch the fisherman; so it can't possibly hurt you."

She gave me a gobletful, and I tasted it. I was satisfied then and wished that they weren't watching me, but I drank it all. It was bitterish, but not very bitter. It had a faint, unpleasant resinous flavor, and a flavor of fetid decaying vegetable matter. But none of these was its chief characteristic. It was a violent astringent. Without causing pain, it puckered the inside of the mouth and the mucous membrane of the throat, like the worst of unripe persimmons. It tasted like stuff that would certainly produce a sharp bellyache, no matter how guiltless one might be.

Presently in fact I began to have a sharp but not agonizing bellyache. The witch-doctor had watched me curiously, nodding his head. I think he saw a strain in my face. He said with kindly, plain intent to reassure me, "You will feel it, but be not afraid. In this matter your heart is pure and it cannot harm you."

So that was what an ordeal by poison was. All those eighteen people sitting around there, guilty or innocent, had, each of them, a sharp bellyache just as I had, and a strained face. Given their belief in the super-added fatal magic element, increase the sharpness of the bellyache, and it seemed to me quite easy to understand how guilty conscience could do the rest, even to the point of causing death in agony—even without the poison *per se* being toxically deadly. Some years ago, it was in Massachusetts I think, a nervous girl in boarding-school died during a mechanically harmless hazing when she was blindfolded and an icicle drawn across her throat.

It was something of this sort, inspired by an individual's guilty fear, which I supposed would now be presently occurring. But at twilight, though they had all drunk again, the strain remained static and torches were brought. Numbers of them were moaning, praying, invoking the Fetich to be done with it. The witch-doctor and Wamba from time to time called loudly on the Fetich. . . .

And then, without warning, the climax came. It came in the form of an agonized screech as a woman, without rising from where she sat, threw herself forward, wallowing and writhing, screaming incoherently upon the ground. And the woman screaming her guilt there, wallowing, begging for mercy, was Fisherman's own wife. What followed quickly now was past my understanding, and they were all too excited, even including Wamba, to take time for explaining. The witch-doctor and Fisherman's angry father bent, questioning the woman, and the father rushed up toward the village, followed by the witch-doctor. They were back in a few minutes and Wamba said, "It was true. They have found it and destroyed it." The others who had drunk were wading meanwhile into the river. Men picked up the writhing woman and took her down into the water. I thought it was an execution, that they were going to drown her. Wamba pushed me toward the water. I saw that they had the woman, holding her so that she could drink, then pounding her on the stomach to make her vomit. They were all drinking and vomiting. Wamba made me drink and vomit too, interminably, until my stomach was cleaned out.

They carried the woman back up into the village and took her into Fisherman's hut, her own hut. Men went in with her. The rest stood outside. It wasn't finished. "What are they going to do with her?" I asked. "You will see," said Wamba. I felt I had reached about the limit of seeing. I was sick at my stomach from the vomiting. Men carried a small log into the hut. Fisherman had gone inside, too. The whole village crowded outside with torches, waiting. From inside the hut came the sound of hacking wood. There was a shuffling, and then a silence. Then the men came out. Only Fisherman and his wife were left inside. From the woman there was not a sound. Presently Fisherman shouted inside, and then came out naked in front of his doorway and showed himself to the crowd, triumphant as a phallic god. The crowd shouted wildly, joyously, leaped dancing round him as if he were indeed a god. He reëntered the silent hut and we went away.

Next morning Wamba and I returned to the big village. I have tried in recounting this affair of Fisherman's bewitchment to suggest margins of possible rationalization for those who have no patience with belief in magic of any sort whatever. But in the late afternoon there came a mild sequel which you may explain or not, as you like. There came, in short, Fisherman with a fine string of fish for my friend Panther-Teeth, newly caught fresh from his fish-traps.

VI

WE WERE back again in the Bin-Hounien territory, welcomed and lodged at Doa, ancestral village of the Yafouba chief San Dei. We had returned to participate in the sacrifices on the tomb of his dead brother, the old chief Bou. Two circumstances now made me more at home here. First, of course, was the presence at my side of Wamba. But second was the simple fact of my returning. I had kept a promise. Few people come from far away to these far places. And almost none return. Etiquette requires the host to say, "You will come again," and you reply, "Yes, I will come again." But if they like you, they are sometimes a little saddened at the parting. They say, dropping etiquette, "You will never come again, but if you ever do you will be welcome."

And if you should return, it is almost always to discover that while you were made to feel at home on the first hospitable occasion, there had been unsuspected curious reticences and withholdings. For example, in this territory there was reputed to be a very difficult and famous witch-doctor, a certain Nago-Ba, whom the old Diagbe, Wamba's cousin, had particularly recommended me to meet and try to talk with. On the first visit I had given San Dei the Diagbe's message and San Dei had promised to transmit it. But next morning he had told me that the Nago-Ba was on a journey.

Now, on the first evening of our present arrival, this Nago-Ba came to our hut, carrying a long silver-headed staff, with a bag of formidable *grigris* hung on his shoulder, impressive, with a face full of wrinkled wisdom, lighted by keen but not unfriendly eyes. He was followed by masks and howlers, came with a pomp as ceremonial as the chief himself. And I thought there was a faint twinkle in his keen old eyes, for on my former visit this Nago-Ba, the great witch-doctor, instead of being absent on a journey, had been present at my elbow all the time, introduced as a poor relation of San Dei's family, seated always humbly on the ground, clothed only in a ragged breech-clout, never once opening his mouth during the whole time I had been in Doa.

Before this second sojourn ended, he may have wished humanly enough that he had still preserved his incognito, for persuaded by Wamba's female flattery and begged humbly by me, he consented to try to teach me something more specific and satisfying than I had yet learned concerning the inner significance of the forest beliefs and the inner meaning of the rites that would occur on the day after the morrow. It was a hard task and it led far afield, for I was trying to get at something basic.

He was patient, but it was slow and difficult, and out of it as we talked late that night and again for a whole morning, there began to emerge a system of metaphysics as idealistic and perhaps as pure, but also just as complicated, as anything ever formulated by Plato and the Greeks or by the Christian saints and mystic theologians. For Nago-Ba here, strange as it may sound with his wooden idols, iron *grigris*, and devil masks, believed that the material world was nothing and that the only ultimate reality was a spiritual reality.

Furthermore his conception of the nature of matter, which he and his forebears had held from immemorial jungle time, was so startlingly parallel with our own newest revolutionary scientific conclusions that one almost asks whether civilized metaphysical science hasn't been simply moving in a circle. Fifty years ago we thought we knew that a stone wall was a stone wall. Now we say that a stone has no material substance whatsoever —in fact that matter as such does not exist—that the only basic unity is a kinetic unity of energy. And just what energy may be in the last abstract, we do not know.

Our half dozen greatest chemists and physicists have, in that non-religious sense, turned completely mystic in their laboratories. With test-tubes and alembics instead of abracadabra and divining-wands, they find themselves knocking again at the door of the infinite. And crazy as it may sound to the casual layman, the concepts held today by advanced science in our greatest universities, concerning the ultimate nature of a stone, of life, of vital energy, of time and spatial dimensions, are closer to the concepts of the black African witch-doctor than to those of our own scientific leaders twenty years ago.

To put down all that this particular witch-doctor said would hopelessly disorganize and interrupt my narrative. Briefly, however, and very briefly, I should like to outline his interesting beliefs on a subject with which concrete science has no direct concern. Since we were going to offer sacrifices to a dead man, I sought to learn from him what doctrine the forest Negro really holds concerning life after death and the nature of the soul. Here then is Nago-Ba's profession of faith, as nearly as I can reproduce it in white terminology:

He believes that every thing which lives, man, beast, insect, tree, and plant, has not only its kinetic vital quality, its life-spark, but a soul quality as well, which is independent both of the body and the vital spark, and hence immortal.

111

(By "soul" and "soul quality," I consider that Nago-Ba means something like "personal essence," like "sentient personality.")

He believes also that every object which we call inanimate, such as a mountain or a stone, likewise a river or plowed field, though lacking any vital spark, is also endowed with this sentient soul quality. His doctrine becomes, therefore, an all-embracing animism.

The soul is the essence and real nature of each thing that exists. The vital spark which a man, beast, or tree has, and a stone has not, is mechanical, soulless, and impersonal. It is like an electric current, a non-sentient blind agent, and the embodied soul's chief busy occupation is guiding it so that it in turn will operate the mechanism of the body. The soul, directing this current, makes the body move and talk, but the body is in reality only a mechanical doll. The *man* himself is neither the mechanical body nor the mechanical current, but an immortal spirit.

When the spark burns out, the mechanical doll is junk and the soul goes free, a disembodied sentient personality. While a man's soul is in his body, or at least so Nago-Ba conceives, he is not worthy of worshiping, of altars or sacrifices, be the man ever so good or seemingly powerful, for the most of his time is taken up selfishly with his own busy mechanical doll job. When it goes free the soul has

not only more power but also more time to occupy itself
with the affairs of others, for helping or harming. Therefore it is wise to keep on favorable terms with such disembodied spirits, and thus simply is derived the Cult of
the Dead, side by side with the nature-worship cult, which
all animist primitives practice.

"Why then," I asked him, "if the soul must go free
from its living envelope to become a cult object, do you
worship a certain tree while it is still living?"

He answered as follows:

"A man's embodied soul is in continual disorder, looking after his disordered body.

"A tree's soul dwells in a more harmonious, better-
adjusted body, and has time already free to occupy itself
with larger matters.

"The soul of a great stone or of a mountain is completely free and has always been so, for the mountain
needs nothing and is always in its place."

To this he added: "The souls of certain ancestors, the
souls of certain great chiefs long dead, sometimes become
as the soul of the mountain."

I asked him one of those unfair, specific questions so
likely to annoy a man who is trying to impart an abstract
doctrine. I asked what he supposed the soul of the old
chief Bou (neither very long dead nor very great, I
judged, in his lifetime) might be busying itself about,

just now, and what precise benefit the family or tribe might derive from the morrow's sacrifice.

He said that one thing Bou might be busying himself with was his own body lying there in the grave, and with his own house in which he doubtless often slept—that it took a longer time than one might think to get rid of old habits, even when one need no longer be bound by them. He would be interested also, however, in whatever might be happening in the village, and was capable of interfering in those happenings, either benevolently or mischievously. Therefore it was very necessary to keep on good terms with him. He might even be listening to us now.

As I was brought up on ghost stories by a South Carolina nurse, and am afraid to this very day of coffins and graveyards except in the sunshine, these last words of Nago-Ba gave the old chief's specter more reality than all the metaphysics and lent the subsequent proceedings a certain spooky plausibility when the time came for marching in procession to the tomb.

This occurred on the following morning. It was neither so pomp-endowed, impressive, or orgiastic as some of the sacrificial ceremonies I had seen in Haiti. It interested me as bearing on the thesis I had presented in my Haitian book, that the gorgeous chorals, processionals, robed priests, litanies, and rituals which characterized and made beautiful the Haitian Petro sacrifice were not of African jungle origin at all, but taken directly from the Roman Catholic Church. Now here indeed the chief difference was that there were neither priests nor formal priestly ritual. Magic is as old as human life. But ritual priestcraft came comparatively late. When Abraham, Isaac, and Jacob offered sacrifice, they themselves or another member of the household built the altar and wielded the knife. Blood and the pious odor of burning flesh sufficed. It was the same for a long while with Ulysses, Agamemnon, and the Greeks. Whether the gods were Yahweh and Satan or Zeus and Pan, it was the same. They had their medicine men, their witch-doctors, long before they had their priests.

Here among the Ivory Coast forest people, the priest had not yet made his appearance, and they still offered sacrifice rudely, as did Abraham and Agamemnon.

The procession formed at an enclosure on the village edge where the sacrificial bull had been penned up. It was a young piebald bull, black and white. It was to be led to the bamboo mausoleum and its throat cut there— by whom? Simply by the village butcher, which gives an important key to the whole ceremony. Rather than partaking in the qualities of a mysterious and holy rite, we were a band bearing gifts to a man who was dead, but doing it very much as if he were a man alive. I, for instance, after consultation with Wamba as to what might be most suitable, carried my last bottle of sparkling Burgundy. She brought white kola nuts wrapped in a packet of green leaves.

The procession which we formed was noisy and not solemn. It was preceded by the tomtom beaters and blowers on ivory trumpets. My bugler Klon, by the chief San Dei's request, was already stationed over yonder at the mausoleum's entrance, sounding his military fanfarrades. If the dead chief's soul were anywhere in the vicinity, either above or under ground, it could hardly fail to hear that brazen summons.

The bull, led by the butcher, was dragged along behind the drums, its flanks slapped and prodded by his assistants. The butcher had strips of green palm leaves tied like bracelets round each wrist. These made his hands the hands of another person, of an unknown man, so that the soul of the bull would not know who had slain it.

San Dei strutted now at our head, sweating under his thick cotton robes and winter European hat of black velours; waving his folded umbrella, surrounded by his howling *griots* who shouted the greatness of the two brothers—the older brother yonder in the tomb, the other who had poisoned him six months before and now came offering pious sacrifice.

I wondered if San Dei had a strip of green palm

twisted round his wrist when he had offered Bou the
fatal cup. I saw gloved fingers tampering with the com-
bination of a safe, then pressing the trigger of an automatic pistol. Did you also protect yourself, San Dei,
against detection by some vague celestial Bertillon? And
is old Bou's soul unaware, as the bull's will be, what
hand hurried it across the mortal threshold? And what
about Bou's son here, already marked for the same exit?

What about him indeed? Nothing surely that any
white could hope to understand, for there he was, the
young chief Yo, who knew that he would soon be sleeping in a smaller tomb beside his father, marching duti-
fully beside us with the classic filial bowl of rice—Black
Hamlet, unrevengeful. What a family! The wives came
following, shaven-headed, their immense brass anklets
clanking like captives from a Piranesi nightmare prison
. . . and then came the crowd.

Bou's tomb, inside its fetich-hung enclosure, was a
simple mound. Arriving there and holding back our lesser
offerings, the bull was dragged in without ceremony of
any sort and thrown upon the mound. Its throat was
slashed wide and deep, the head almost severed, and the
blood gushed enormously. I was surprised to see how
much blood the earth could drink up, and how quickly.
The earth is always thirsty for more blood. Hills of
Verdun, abattoirs, and altars. There was even once a little

hill outside Jerusalem. But the earth is never satisfied.

The old dead chief, however, was well pleased, I hoped, with the good gifts we brought him. The bowls of rice, of fruit, of oil, the fine white kola nuts, were laid there piously and seemed as likely to please a dead man as flowers, ribbons, terra-cotta wreaths, cast-iron crosses. With Wamba's help, holding a stone, I knocked off the neck of my last wine-bottle and offered its contents to the dead chief, as I had offered wine a few weeks earlier to San Dei, his living brother.

We went outside the enclosure to where the crowd was waiting and San Dei made a speech. It was a curious discourse, addressed partly to his people and partly to the dead man. He puffed, strutted, and became oratorical, pacing up and down as he spoke, perspiring, and gesticulating with his umbrella, like a United States senator canvassing in rural districts. First he reviewed ancestral family glories and tribal prosperity; then pronounced a long encomium on the strength and virtues of the dead chief Bou, addressing him in the first person. He assured Bou that he had been a great chief, an elephant in war and a mighty voice in counsel. All had trembled before him and he had been first among men. He had been the husband of all the younger men, who had been as women compared with him. (Well then, San Dei, my friend, I wondered, if all that is true, how are you going to ex-

118

plain why you put him under ground? Or is that a point
on which to preserve a polite silence?) But there I did
him an injustice. He was leading up to it. Bou had been
the strongest and the wisest, he proclaimed, but being
chief was a hard job, and Bou, it seemed, had eventually
begun to get old and tired. Having ruled so well and for
so many years, he deserved to be relieved of the burden.
In short he hoped that Bou would understand—San Dei
was still addressing him directly—that they had really
done him a loving favor in poisoning him, and that he
should be grateful and still help them in the spirit world.
Surely he must realize that everything had been done
for the best.

Of course it wasn't quite so definitely expressed as this,
but since the whole tribe had been in a sense San Dei's
accomplices, every one understood what he was talking
about and deemed it a wise discourse.

Yo also had been listening with a respectful and profound attention, but it seemed to me that in applauding
he was a shade less enthusiastic than the others. He was
not, however, during the time I knew him, very enthusiastic about anything—a fact scarcely to be wondered at
under all the circumstances.

The bull was being butchered there in the sunshine
and pieces distributed to notables and heads of families.
An old poor man whose family held the special privilege

119

like a knighthood in payment for some ancestral act of prowess, danced for the entrails and carried them away in a huge basket. Feasting and banghi drinking lasted all the afternoon and long into the night.

The evening of the day which followed brought a strange experience, the most difficult and unsatisfactory experience of this whole African adventure. I dislike even to approach it. To a more open, credulous, and believing mind, it might easily have been the climax, the great high spot. To a tight mind, anesthetic *a priori* toward all seeming marvels, it could have been arbitrarily dismissed as a piece of amazing trickery. But my mind had no pigeon-hole in which it could be made to fit. I had wanted desperately to see it, but I realized immediately after I had seen it that it left me unsatisfied and at a loss, and although many months have now elapsed it leaves me at a complete loss still.

It involved, of course, the business of the children pierced by swords. Wamba had been able to persuade them where I had not. The two baby girls and the jugglers had been summoned, and had been shut up all day secretly in the witch-doctor's enclosure. Night came and we gathered in the torch-lighted public compound. The big village crowd, the natives themselves, were nervous, quiet, and almost as if terrorized. There were old ones who said it ought not to be done. I remembered what San Dei had said on the former occasions when they had refused to do it: "There is real magic. But it is dangerous. The recovery does not always take place." The two children, impassive as if drugged, but able to stand and move about, open-eyed like somnambulists, were brought out by the jugglers. And then whatever it was that happened, happened.

There is a personal problem involved here, and not a new problem, but one which as a writer I have hitherto consistently evaded. I feel that I should not evade it any longer, but how to approach it is very difficult.

Epictetus points out that although a man is wiser than a sheep, a decent sheep doesn't eat a lot of grass and then spit it out in the others' faces to astonish them by showing how much grass it has eaten, but digests it internally and in due season produces externally milk and wool.

In this case I have only undigested grass to offer, and it is not the first time I have fed on strange herbs in indigestible pastures. But on former occasion I have kept my mouth shut afterward, and I ask personally forgiveness now on the part of my readers for approaching with this awkwardness and hesitation a subject which worries me so greatly.

A good many years ago, tramping in an Italian mountain district where peasants were steeped in the elder traditions of pre-Christian sorcery, I saw a thing happen which cannot happen. It was my first experience of the sort. It was a long time ago. But I have never written about it (though I have written freely enough concerning other forms of magic), and I have never told about it to more than three or four special people. Something in the texture of my mind balks not merely at telling the thing, but at the thing itself. Similar problems, on a few rare occasions—personal to me and also involving what I ought to write—arose in Arabia, in Kurdistan and Haiti. I could arrive at no conclusion and completely eliminated every reference to them in the text. To me they present an insoluble dilemma, because on the one hand *I do not believe in miracles, or that magic can produce physical materialized phenomena of any sort whatever;* and on the other hand *I am convinced that in the face of certain phenomena, no hypothesis of charlatan trickery is any good either.*

What then, you ask, remains for me to offer as an observer in the present case? Undigested grass, an indecent offering, which I surely ask no other man to accept as nourishment. I include it because of a feeling that my former reticences may trace partly to a contemptible prudence, and because it represents a part of the composite picture of so-called black magic in West Africa.

All the bad fiction-traditional stage props were there—night, torchlight, superstition, crowds hysterical, and mumbo-jumbo raised to its nth power. Anything like laboratory control was nonsense. Yet the ordinary hypotheses of trickery (I know them all: group hypnotism, substitution of simulacres, puppets introduced by sleight-of-hand, etc., etc.) were simply no good in the face of the close visual and tactile evidence. For there were the two living children, close to me. I touched them with my hands. They were three-dimensional warm flesh. And there equally close, to be touched and seen, were the two men with their swords. The swords were iron, three-dimensional, metal, cold and hard. And this is what I now *saw* with my eyes, but you will understand why I am reluctant to tell of it and that I do not know what *seeing* means:

Each man, holding his sword stiffly upward with his left hand, tossed a child high in air with his right, then caught it full upon the point, impaling it like a butterfly on a pin. No blood flowed, but the two children were there, held aloft, pierced through and through, impaled upon the swords. The crowd screamed now, falling to its knees. Many veiled their eyes with their hands, and others fell prostrate. Through the crowd the jugglers marched, each bearing a child aloft, impaled upon his sword, and disappeared into the witch-doctor's enclosure.

My first mental reaction, purely automatic, was that I had seen jugglery turn suddenly to ritual murder. But whatever had happened, it was not that. I was assured that in an hour or more, "if things didn't go wrong," we would see and touch the children, alive and well. For once I said nothing at all to Wamba. I knew there was nothing she could tell me that I could believe or understand. I had no doubt that the children might reappear alive, but my mind had reached its old balking point. I would reject the evidence of my senses rather than accept literally a physical miracle, and I believe I shall do so until I die. I believe that if I had been the apostle Thomas and touched with my own hands the wounds of Christ, I should have remained a doubter still in miracles. And thus it was—please understand I mean no silly blasphemy but am trying to make clear something very difficult—that when these two children were brought out presently, and I touched them, and they were still warm flesh, it convinced me of nothing whatsoever, except that there may perhaps be elements in this unholy jungle sorcery, just as there were unknown elements perhaps in the recorded holier miracles of other days, which transcend what science knows of natural law, but not our possibility of ultimate knowledge.

Let me state this paradox and be done with it. I may some day conceivably be forced to believe, if the evidence is strong enough, that a man has walked through a stone wall, or been wafted up into the clouds, or that he has been changed into a fox, or even that he has belatedly arisen from the dead after he began to rot like Lazarus. But admitting the factual occurrence, I will still deny that a miracle has occurred. And for this, of course, if I am wrong, I will be damned.

Wamba said I was wrong, but with all her wisdom she could not help me further. She said that if I consented to remain there always, and give up everything, including even my white ways of asking, she might eventually make me understand, but that it would be a road from which there could be no returning.

Her words were painful to me, and familiar. But they were the words which only saints or madmen, the very wise or the very simple, have ever truly dared to follow.

So we occupied ourselves with other matters, and on a day there was leave-taking, and I went away into the country of the Gueré.

PART TWO

CANNIBALS

I

EXCEPT that he wore a French fireman's helmet instead of the classic high silk hat, the cannibal king Mon-Po, my first host among the Gueré, was quite in the best tradition of the cannibal kings we have all known and been fond of since childhood in the comic weeklies and the Katzenjammer Sunday papers.

That is to say, he was a somewhat funny fellow, and sympathetic. He was on excellent terms with the nearest French administrator—since there existed a sort of gentleman's agreement that he wouldn't eat wandering black corporals or casual white strangers. No agreement was necessary concerning missionaries—since in the Gueré territory there are no longer any missionaries.

But aside from these two lacks—no missionaries and no opera hats—the Gueré measured up to all my cherished expectations. Just why the cannibal *per se* has, among other qualities, a certain pleasing, humorous, and sympathetic aspect for the young folks and old folks at home, is a queer point in civilized psychology. Even my

darling little Grandmother Buehler, who smelt of lavender and contributed regularly to foreign missions, would
smile back at the smiling cannibal who stood beaming
expansively on a clerical gentleman with umbrella and
hymnbook, in close proximity to a large iron pot. Nearly
all mild old ladies in rocking-chairs, as well as children,
including sweet little girls, delight in these perennial
whimsies in which the joke is that the plump bishop will
presently be had for dinner.

When I told Carl Helm of the New York *Sun* that I
had heard of a real cannibal tribe in Africa and was hoping to live with them for a while, he also broke immediately into a broad grin, and wrote subsequently a very
funny sympathetic story about it. Returning to Paris,
the first question all my French friends asked me, and
always with smiles, was whether I had succeeded in living
among the cannibals, and what recipes I had brought
back. Why this attitude exists, I do not know, but hap-
pily for me it does exist, so that I may venture to hope
that while people may think I carry curiosity to crazy
extremes, they will not consider it necessary to take steps
toward having me locked up in jail or put in an insane
asylum.

For the fact is that I have brought back, among other
things, a number of recipes of which I can speak with
substantial authority.

CANNIBALS

It will be better, I think, to have this clear at the start before launching on the general tale of my adventure in the Gueré country. One of my chief purposes in going to Africa was to see and meet and live with cannibals. Even aside from their delightful humorous aspect, they are a highly interesting and wholly legitimate subject, whether for the adventurer or the learned anthropologist. A great many books have been written about cannibals by learned and worthy people, and more recently a great many cannibal films have been turned. They are all disappointing, books and films alike, because they invariably evade at last the central issue in the sense that they offer no first-hand observation or experience on the one essential dietetic point that makes the difference between a cannibal and my grandmother. And it seemed impossible, furthermore, for me or any one to offer anything better unless one actually knew what one was talking about with reference to the one precise thing that makes a cannibal a cannibal.

I present the issue here fairly at the outset, because in what will follow somewhat later, I honestly do not want to shock or distress any one. I made up my mind before leaving New York that when it came to the subject of cannibals I would either write nothing whatever about them, or I would know what I was writing about. It is really too dull to sit through a long book or film about cannibals only to learn at the end that the guests after all did not remain for dinner. I think it may be proper to add here that I posed the abstract issue to a sincere priest who, aside from his ecclesiastical functions, has made valuable contributions to ethnology; also to a well-known professor of pragmatic philosophy; also to a doctor of exceptional distinction and integrity. They discussed it candidly, and were all of the same opinion that it would be of legitimate physiological and ethnological interest if one could learn, by actually dining off it once at any rate, why cannibals prefer the meat of *homo sapiens* to that of other animals.

Arriving then finally among the Gueré, I broached this subject at the earliest opportunity, and since they were proud of being cannibals, they were quite willing to consider it with perfect freedom. But some time necessarily elapsed before I had personal opportunity to verify their statements.

Not only were they themselves proud of being cannibals, as distinguished from weaker neighboring tribes like the Ouabé and Yafouba, but the French Ivory Coast officials, in a certain humorous and of course unofficial way, were proud of them too—a pride which did not prevent them, however, from jailing and condemning occasional individuals who, as they would say, "exaggerated"—that is, overstepped the bounds of discretion in selecting their candidates for the cook-pot, and let themselves get caught afterward.

This paradoxical pride in a thing which officially they were doing their honest best to stamp out was of course a light thing, own cousin to my grandmother's smile. But as far up as Timbuctoo later in the year, officials would grin and say, "Oh, yes, Colbert and his cannibals!" And then, more than likely, they would ask, "What about old Tei? Is he still in the calaboose?"

This Colbert, though a youth, administered a forest district bigger than one of our average eastern States and inhabited exclusively by the Gueré tribes. While doing all in his power to maintain law and order, he liked his cannibals, and they liked him—so well, in fact, that they often voluntarily brought their troubles to him for judgment. He lived alone, the only white for nearly fifty miles around, at a village administration post called Blengi.

As for Tei, he was a cannibal chief who had got himself jailed and famous because he had eaten his young wife, a handsome, lazy wench called Blito, along with a dozen of her girl friends, and had then enacted such a roaring farce at the expense of the French military detachment first sent in to arrest him that something simply had to be done about it. He was in jail then, not so much for cannibalism as for greediness and for subsequently making monkeys of the authorities.

Since young Colbert and his cannibals were famous in West Africa, where there are very few real cannibal tribes left, the thing to do, everybody told me, was to go to Blengi and see Colbert. The post itself could be reached, it seemed, by motor road; that is, if no recent herd of elephants had torn it up, for this was also the heart of the big elephant country. We sent him word a week in advance, and after various trivial vicissitudes arrived safely one afternoon—Katie, my black chauffeur Yao, and our little Citroën truck piled high with camp junk, bars of salt, and what not.

One never knows what one may find at the end of a road in the forest. But this time, traversing a small mud village, we drove into a superb compound garden, flowers, orange and lemon trees, elephant skulls immense like monuments at angles of the lawn, a table with colored umbrella that suggested tea in the Bois de Boulogne, a great rambling thatched house with luxurious veranda— and from the veranda to meet us, a grinning, clean-shaven young chap in sport pajamas and sun helmet.

Ten minutes later we were sprawling in deck chairs, drinking lemonade with a dash of vermouth, listening to Stravinsky's *Firebird*, and liking Monsieur Colbert very much indeed. He had Paris newspapers and magazines two months old, with items concerning people and things in which we were mutually interested. There was a second house in a corner of the garden which he proposed to put at our disposal, and as for my becoming later the guest of a cannibal king, he announced, grinning and with a certain pride, that he had convoked four of his best ones for the following morning so that I could meet them and take my choice. In fact I could go and visit all of them in the bush if I wanted to. He would put hammocks and porters at my disposal for as long as I liked.

Next morning he sent coffee to our bedside, and when we dressed lazily and strolled out into the garden, there sat the four cannibal kings in chairs in a row on the lawn, like bad little boys invited to a birthday party, wearing their best Sunday manners and their best Sunday clothes. They had come from afar, from four corners of the forest, where each ruled a separate division of the Guéré tribe.

Colbert, who treated them with a humorous friendliness not altogether lacking in respect—an attitude toward petty native potentates which Anglo-Saxon colonists seem neither capable nor desirous of achieving—introduced them as his "dear colleagues," paid them compliments, and asked tenderly after the health of their families.

135

The oldest was a fattish man named Tao (which meant, they told me, Welcome). He wore a mandarin-shaped hat, some clanking chains with bells on them, and a piece of panther skin which kept slipping from his shoulder.

The second was a powerful, rather brutal-looking chief named Blia-Eddo (which meant Old Villager). He wore a black cap of monkey fur and striped robes.

The third, named Gedao (which meant the Torch, or the Flame), was a sinewy serious-looking old-fashioned fellow with a scraggly beard and teeth filed to points, who made no compromises in favor of modern styles. He wore bones and ivory sticks in his braided hair and a leather thong round his middle, from which two scanty strips of cloth hung down before and behind.

The fourth—I am really saving him for the last because he pleased me most and later became a friend— was he of the shiny fireman's helmet. His name was Mon-Po (which meant the one who must not die). He was a muscular little man, past his prime, with a wily, funny face, and for some reason he seemed to think that Katie was just as funny as he was. She was, incidentally, the first white woman he had ever seen. They both laughed when they shook hands, as if they had a secret. Mon-Po examined a wisp of her hair with his fingers and then patted her in several spots, combining a doggish friendliness with an evident naïve desire to estimate how plump she was—not, one suspected, as a problematical candidate for the cook-pot, but rather for his harem. This Mon-Po was a notorious lady's man, so Colbert told us, and already had some forty wives.

Bottles and a table were brought by servants as at a garden party in France, and we clinked glasses with the four little cannibal kings, discussing with Colbert which of them I might visit first, and how. He made a pencil sketch of the surrounding country in which he himself was the big king or overlord.

And what a kingdom! Here we sat on a lawn, with tables, bottles, a white-coated butler—not to mention the veranda where the night before over coffee and liqueurs we had seen a first-edition Rimbaud, talked of mutual acquaintances in Paris, discussed Joyce and Gide, listened to modernist music. And now we might have been on a garden terrace between Nice and Monte Carlo. But it was crazy like an American newspaper comic page or a farcical operetta because of the four fantastic guests who sat there with us. It became even more fantastic as Colbert talked. We were in the center of a jungle, cut through by one single motor road, a jungle territory bigger than an average French department or a State in New England, most of it entirely unmapped, lying between great rivers, and with certain sections, bigger than average

counties, into which no white man had ever yet penetrated. Five miles off the road, in any direction, lay
jungle mystery. From where we sat, we might—though
it happened we did not—hear herds of elephants crashing
through to the river. Colbert brought a military map and
showed us totally blank spots big enough to make a minor
European principality. He told us how his guards one
day had brought in, wound round with a rope, a stark
naked black man with matted hair, who walked like a
gorilla, made animal noises, and spoke no known language or dialect. He had come out of the bush and frightened a woman on the edge of a village near the big road.
The villagers had taken him and turned him over to Colbert's guards. When led before Colbert, the man just
laughed and shook his ropes and made animal noises.
"What could I do?" said Colbert. "There was no reason
for putting him in jail. And I couldn't very well keep
him in a cage. There wasn't anything to do. I had them
take him to the edge of the forest and turn him loose as
you would a bird or a wild animal." He accompanied this
with a wide gesture and added, "Every three months I
get colonial forms printed in Paris to be filled out with
detailed statistics on agriculture and population in my
territory—including white European population, deaths,
births, etc. *Eh bien*, within a radius of fifty miles from
where we sit, there are exactly four white men and no

white women. And as for the last European who died here, so far as I know, it was an American commercial elephant hunter named Anderson. That was in 1917, I think. At any rate it was before I came. Old Gedao, the Torch, there, can tell you more about that story than I can. The American became unpopular with his guides; so they killed him and ate him. It happened in Gedao's territory; so the administration gave Gedao a rifle and put it up to him. Ten days later he brought in the heads of the three principal guides. He had stalked and got them himself, one by one. That old fellow is not the chief of his tribe for nothing. Look at him. He knows what we are talking about, and he's proud."

I had taken a strong fancy to Mon-Po, he of the fire helmet, and Colbert recommended that after I had visited him, it might be well to go and stop a while also with Gedao. He made them all an extravagant speech about me, and they responded with extravagantly polite invitations. They departed with gifts, including a bushel of Colbert's oranges, which the forest blacks do not know how to cultivate, and a quantity of my bar salt.

After luncheon, Colbert sent for a young Guéré gentleman named Diisi, whom he proposed generously to lend me as guide and adviser. Diisi was a lucky choice despite the fact that he had been three years to school in Senegal and spoke both French and English as well as a quantity of native dialects. He looked like a Columbia student, wore patent leather shoes, had a fountain pen and note-book, but he was all right. While Katie retired for a siesta, and Colbert to work on his reports, I wandered off with Diisi into the village to arrange about the porters, and also, if I could persuade him, to consult his grand-father's arm.

Colbert had told us about Diisi's grandfather's arm at luncheon. Every local Gueré who planned doing anything important always consulted Diisi's grandfather's arm, paying Diisi a price for the privilege, and Diisi himself never made any vital decision without first communing with it.

So I explained to him that I had always consulted the Fetiches and sacrificed to them in Yafouba territory, and that I would feel much safer and happier among the Gueré if we first obtained his defunct grandfather's coun-sels and benediction. Diisi, doubtless quite sincere, but also knowing certainly that I would not go empty-handed to the family shrine, was pleased as any village priest in Brittany when a traveler pays for a special mass in the local chapel.

This present chapel was a hut in Diisi's family com-pound. The arm and hand of his grandfather, dried, hard and black as ebony, was no more repellent than any other anatomical sacred relic such as one may see by the hun-

dreds in similar shrines in Christian Europe. It hung
suspended like a pendulum by a long cord from the
peaked thatch roof. It hung above a flat stone altar
which was bare, but *ex voto* offerings in profusion decked
the walls of the hut—bracelets, leather *grigris*, wooden
agricultural tools, articles of clothing, bows and arrows,
spears, an old rusty flintlock musket.

Diisi explained that when a man or woman contemplated a dangerous or important act, such as going to
hunt the panther, elephant, or crocodile, planting a new
field, marrying, or going on a journey, they would place
upon the altar some object connected with the enterprise,
and after a while, if his grandfather was favorable, the
arm would sway above it, impregnating the instrument
with virtue, and would sometimes give valuable indica-
tions or counsels. Sometimes also, he said, they laid sick
babies on the stone.

I asked what he thought I had best deposit there, and
he reflected. Some article of clothing, he suggested, and
my shoes, since we were going on a journey; and perhaps
some object of intimate daily use. So I took off my shoes
and stripped off my shirt and laid them in a neat pile
and placed on top of them a pencil stub with some notes
I had been making. The pencil stub seemed rightest since
it was my only workman's tool.

Diisi talked to his grandfather as if the old man were

present in the room with us, offering filial greeting, introducing me respectfully, explaining that we were going
on a friendly visit to the remote villages. Then we sat
down on a mat, and to my slight surprise Diisi lighted
a cigarette. It always surprises me slightly when people
treat their gods and spooks familiarly. He crossed his
legs, spat on the floor, offered me a light, made himself
comfortable, said one could never tell about his grandfather; we might have to wait a long time.

Considering the manner in which the arm was suspended, I was only mildly astonished, if at all, when,
after not too long a time, it began to sway gently as if
in friendly benediction above my poor belongings. I was
pleased as when one sees a lot of rabbits come out of a
hat, and Diisi was pleased perhaps more piously, for he
said that sometimes the arm jerked and jiggled to express his grandpapa's disapproval. A friendly breeze stirring the thatch peak, or a friendly ghost? Why insist?
It was friendly, and Diisi and I would both feel happier,
more friendly toward each other, and more confident on
our journey.

I asked if I might hang some offering upon the wall.
He said no, not yet; I should promise now, and do it on
our safe return. Grandpapa, it seemed, must earn the
reward before he got it. I thought how when Aubrey and
I were lost at night in the Haitian mountains, we loudly

promised twelve gilded candles to Saint Christopher if he would bring us safe to shelter. Candles might now be sent to me from Man. Katie was returning to Man and could arrange it.

So I said: "O Grandfather of Diisi and Grandfather of the Guéré, be good to us, watch over us, and on our return you shall have a fine illumination as well as something nice to hang upon your wall."

Behind the altar, on a sort of ledge under the roof, in the shadows, I had observed a number of old human skulls, and two smaller ones which I had thought at first were skulls of children, but which seemed on looking closer to be the skulls of chimpanzees. I asked Diisi to tell me about them if telling were not forbidden. He said no, that it was not forbidden, that it was a family matter but known to all. The ancestral food-taboo of his family, he explained, was the flesh of man and the flesh of the chimpanzee, which no member of his family must ever eat. Every family group in the forest has a food-taboo of some sort. One family may never eat the flesh of goats; for another the buffalo or hippo is taboo; for still another family it may be a certain grain or fruit. And for each family the taboo thing which must not be eaten is also protective and Fetich. The family which may not eat rice, for instance, will have dried sheaves of rice upon its altars, and the family which may not eat a certain

143

animal will piously conserve its skull or bones and hold them in veneration.

In the days before the French came, Diisi told me, when there was a special feast here in the village, and the choice parts were distributed to notable families, his family could not participate, but after the feasting the skull was brought to them. Neither Diisi himself nor any of his ancestors, though a family of chiefs and pure-blood Gueré, had ever tasted flesh of man or great ape.

I asked him what he could tell me of cannibal customs now in the Gueré bush. He said that times had greatly changed and become somewhat "corrupt" since the arrival of the white man's government, because the whites could not always understand the difference between honest cannibals and criminals like the Panther societies, for instance. There was less honest inter-tribal raiding, he said, than there used to be—almost no inter-tribal wars, and consequently honest meat was rarer. The entire Gueré group, it seemed, were traditionally warrior-cannibals, but since the whites discountenanced even honest fighting, some of the group, he candidly admitted, had degenerated. The proper honest cannibals, that is, the fighting cannibals, I gathered from Diisi's talk, had a sort of code of honor of their own, and also their "game laws," prescribed by themselves before the whites ever came.

Men slain in battle or in village raids were legitimate

game, he said, and likewise the hostile or unfriendly neighbor ambushed and taken on the trail. But to kill one's own for food, or to kill the wayfaring stranger who came legitimately in peace or for a friendly purpose, as for instance the black Dioula trader, was simply murder as the white man understands murder, and was so regarded by the Gueré and punished by themselves before the French ever entered the Ivory Coast.

Today, said Diisi quaintly, a certain amount of honest old-fashioned cannibalism still goes on, but those cases are precisely the ones that never reach the official ears of the administration. The only cases which result in arrests and trials are the cases which the Gueré themselves, if honest men, regard as criminal and themselves denounce —for instance, the case of Tei, who slaughtered his own wife; and the nine Panther Men in prison at Guglio, convicted for murdering people in their own villages, and denounced finally by their own black neighbors.

I have heard certain travelers, both American and French, assert roundly that African cannibal stories today are cock-and-bull stories—that there is no cannibalism any longer in West Africa. It may interest them to know that in the districts of Man, Douékué, and Guglio alone, a central forest section of the Côte l'Ivoire, Afrique Occidentale Française, there have been twenty-six formal convictions in the past five years (accompanied in most cases by final complete confessions), of which seven occurred in the year of our Lord 1929. Unfortunately, being Panther Society and criminal murder cases in which the victim is eaten incidentally, their records do not shed much light on the customs or psychology of the self-respecting cannibal who enjoys with a good appetite and healthy conscience the enemy cut down in ambush or fair fighting.

I had access to the records of all these trials, reams of red tape documents, which would make a book in themselves, but what Diisi told me as we sat and smoked cigarettes in his grandfather's chapel—on the eve of going into the bush—seemed much more important and interesting.

II

The *griot* Sibley sang:

> *He has thirty-nine wives,*
> *Their necks are like giraffes;*
> *Their breasts are always full of milk,*
> *And they are always pregnant.*

Pointing to Fire Helmet, he paused, filled his lungs with air, and shouted:

> *He is the great bull buffalo*
> *Alone in the bush.*
> *He is M'Blo, the joy of his wives,*
> *And the terror of elephants.*
> *His horn is the mightiest.*

Sibley was a handsome man with a head like the statue of Augustus Caesar. He wore a plaid golf cap, and nothing else whatever. The taste of cannibals in head-gear has always been spectacularly catholic.

As for my host Fire Helmet, in addition to his shining *casque-de-pompier*, he had donned a superb leather crazy-

147

JUNGLE WAYS

quilt smock, painted and embroidered in every color of
the rainbow, and he sat beside a magnificently carved
war drum ten feet tall. It was the morning of my arrival
in his village. A long-cherished, almost childhood project
had been realized. I was a guest of the cannibals, apparently on good terms with them, with a hut in the village,
and permission to remain as long as I liked. It was perfectly apparent too that my excellent Yafouba friends
were bush-leaguers compared to these Gueré. Their
thatched houses were bigger and better built, there were
more evidences of prosperity in the village, the king's
entourage was more savagely elaborate. He was attended
by a group of young women, high-breasted, naked Ama-
zons bearing long polished staves, old counselors with
headdresses of green leaves, devil dancers whose monstrous masks were brilliantly painted and surmounted
with fur and feathers.

The entire village was crowded round, watching us.
The men were the huskiest and the women the most
beautiful I had thus far seen in Africa. They were, in
short, a traditionally fighting tribe, hospitable, prosperous, and proud as blazes. They had been great slavers in
their time, raiding their less warlike neighbors, taking
their captives down the Sassandra in long wooden dug-
outs to where the white slave ships waited. They still had
wealth of ancient bells, chains, beads, hand-wrought iron

148

weapons, and utensils centuries old from Europe that would have made the fortune of an antique shop in New York or Paris.

Fire Helmet jumped up frequently from his chair, gesticulating, shouting orders. He was a wiry little chap, smaller in stature than most of his warriors, but cocky as a bantam rooster, almost too cocky, like a man acting a rôle, overdoing self-confidence, a comedian and tyrannical. It pleased me that while he and the rest of them were perfectly friendly, even gay, there was no obsequiousness in their attitude. Even the compliments of the *griot* Sibley were far from naïve, and amiably ambiguous. After proclaiming with many flourishes and variations that the Gueré were the greatest and the strongest *ad infinitum*, he turned to me and said, in parenthesis, as one intelligent man to another, "Of course we know that the whites are now stronger than the blacks—but that is a wholly different subject."

And the very first evening over the banghi drinking, Fire Helmet, after some side questions to my friend Diisi, wanted to know why I hadn't brought Katie along and whether I would consider selling her. I wasn't sure and I'm not sure yet whether he was joshing me. So I replied politely that the idea had never precisely occurred to me.

The dinner we had that night was unquestionably chicken and rice, and the late luncheon next day was unquestionably excellent goat *en brochette*, garnished with bananas and pepper pods. Also there was palm wine in abundance. Differently from the Yafouba custom, where by their own tacit wish I had eaten apart, I was always Fire Helmet's table guest, the table consisting of a mat spread under a tree in his compound. Sibley, Diisi, and two or three of his counselors usually ate with us, served by several of Fire Helmet's wives. The food was in iron pots and calabash bowls. We used knives, big iron spoons, and our fingers.

As mealtime seemed a polite and appropriate time for conversation touching their more special local menus and cuisine, I approached it from an angle one evening by asking Fire Helmet casually if he had ever eaten white meat. He looked at me quizzically and laughed as if it were as good a joke as any. He said he had eaten it rarely in his youth, and hadn't tasted it for nearly twenty years; that it tasted exactly like the meat of the black man, and was no better; that since the French had established themselves and made peace, the white man was no longer an enemy. Anyway, he added with another grin, the whites had always been too difficult to catch, and they made too many bothersome histories about it afterward. So it really wasn't worth the bother. It tasted in no way different, he repeated, from the meat of the black man.

So! And how precisely did that taste?

CANNIBALS

Here at last was a chance for preliminary talk with a man who really knew what he was talking about, on a subject concerning which I had never either heard or read anything first-hand or convincing.

The "long pig" stories repeated or published on hearsay from anonymous shipwrecked South Sea sailors and equally apocryphal African traders long since dead have been the most persistent and consistent of these tales at second hand. "And he said," or "and he told me," that "it looked and smelled and tasted exactly like pork." Such stories have always seemed to have a strong *a priori* likelihood of being true, because the taste of any meat depends to a certain degree on the sort of diet the animal itself eats, and the pig and the man are two of the rare mammals who notoriously eat more or less anything and everything. Most mammals are herbivores, eating only grass and grain, or carnivores, eating only flesh. But man and pig eat everything from dandelions and cornmeal mush to tripe, green cheese, and caviar. Therefore, in theorizing academically it would seem reasonable enough to guess that, eaten in their turn, the meat of the animal man might closely resemble the meat of the animal pig.

This academic likelihood was running through my mind when I asked Fire Helmet how, precisely, did human flesh taste?

His replies, alas, were not very illuminating. They

were frank but not instructive. He said with conviction that it was "very good meat," and seeing that I was not satisfied, insisted with even stronger conviction that "it was as good meat as any, and was considered by some people to be the best meat of all."

Decidedly that didn't help any. It was even less instructive than books and tales which I had scorned. And since I didn't entirely scorn them but had in mind their theoretical probability, I said, to help him toward some possible comparison, "Have you ever eaten pork? Does it taste anything like pork?"

He said, "But it tastes nothing like pork. It isn't like pork at all. It isn't the same thing at all. We have pigs here in the village. I have often eaten pork. It is not anything like that."

Alas, alas! Hearsay contradicting hearsay. And then what? That would be a fine thing to take home and put into a book. It would be even worse than the others.

"But what flesh does it resemble most?" I insisted. "Is it like goat, or sheep, or beef, or dog?"

He puzzled over it, shaking his head. Obviously there was only one thing to do, if I ever could, and I didn't know him well enough or trust Diisi's discretion sufficiently to broach my wish directly. But we still talked on. Fire Helmet, shaking his head, and getting perhaps a little bored by my interminable questions, said finally that he would send for the old tribal chief cook who lived at some distance in another village and who could probably give me better answers. At any rate he could tell me something about the cuisine, in which I was likewise interested.

So we let the matter drop for a number of days while I settled down with them, lived and played, drank banghi, and got better acquainted. The early explorers whose books on Africa are now more or less classic have nearly all observed that the traditional cannibal tribes were usually the most powerful and prosperous, and incidentally the most hospitable. I found this to be still true in general of the Gueré. They seemed stronger and better proportioned physically than their tamer forest neighbors. They wore fewer clothes, the majority of both men and women going naked except for ornaments and loincloths, although most of the notables and a considerable minority of the rest wore scattering garments and nondescript headgear of filtered-in Soudanese or European origin. Their houses consisted usually of one large circular living-room, mud-walled, bamboo-ceilinged, with a notch-stick ladder and trapdoor leading to an attic storeroom under the peak-thatched roof. Their beds were sometimes grass mats, sometimes cots made with bamboo poles and leather thongs. Cooking and household utensils combined native calabash and wooden objects with iron pots, knives, spoons, sometimes even enamelware bowls and cups from Europe. In clearings near the village and farther away beside the river they cultivated rice, millet, cooking-bananas, and patates. They had goats, sheep, chicken in abundance; a few pigs and cattle, which thrive poorly in the forest. They took fish, crocodile, and hippo from the Sassandra and game from the bush, usually with spears, nets, traps, bows and arrows, but a few special hunters had muzzle-loading muskets, wound round with rawhide to keep them from exploding under heavy charge. They bought lead from Dioula traders, but made their own gunpowder (a trick learned probably from the old trade contacts with white slavers) from charcoal and from saltpeter procured by boiling and rendering earth impregnated with the urine of their sheep and goats. In religion they were animist-Fetichers like all their neighbors. They were generally polygamous, and wives represented chattel wealth.

Girls were bought and sold as one chose, but were not slaves. Health, youth, and beauty determined values, ranging up from two or three sheep to a number of cattle. A very high price would be a value equivalent to fifteen or twenty dollars. Virginity except as a concomitant of youth and health was deemed of no particular importance, but wives once bought must be virtuous.

They offered me my choice of a number of pretty girls,

but I temporized. Old Fire Helmet couldn't understand this, for he had ladies on the brain. He was never more cocky than when talking about it or when the *griot* Sibley made up some extravagant new song about his prowess as a great bull buffalo. This seemed somewhat queer in a black man, for usually, though they take their sex seriously, they take it naturally and simply and do not brag.

One night Fire Helmet sent word by Diisi that he wanted to see me alone for a very private conference. It was one of the most absurd, wholly unlikely, and in a way amusing things that ever happened to me in Africa. We went surreptitiously, almost like conspirators, to Fire Helmet's rambling, rectangular mud-thatched "palace" and found him seated all alone on some panther skins in a windowless little inner cubby-hole of a room. It was evidently a sort of "den" or private study into which he retired to contemplate grave matters.

He seemed a bit embarrassed. He seemed also to be talking at random. He asked if I were enjoying myself and said he hoped I would stay a long time. Did I want to go and visit some panther traps with him next day? The medicine I had given various sick ones in the village (it had been mostly the simplest of remedies, purgative pills, aspirin, and quinine) had worked marvels, he said, and they were all delighted. The old cook would be coming along soon and would give me all the information I wished, etc., etc. But what the devil was he leading up to? He returned again to the subject of my medicines. The whites had powerful medicaments for everything. At last he was coming to the point. The truth of the matter was, he said, that he was not so very young, and thirty-nine wives were a great many, and he was sure that if I were as well-wishing a friend of his as I seemed to be, with my medicine chest that contained everything, I ought to be able to do something about that too.

In a word, or rather in a good many round-about words, the Great Bull Buffalo, the Terror of Elephants, the Joy of His Wives, was confiding to me that he was not the man he once had been. No one had cast a spell on him, he said. He was simply tired and getting old.

I was flattered to be taken into his confidence. I was also amused and shamelessly well disposed to do anything I could to please or help him, but somewhat embarrassed because so far as I am aware—outside of cantharides, which is merely a local irritant and of which I naturally had none anyway—there is no such thing as an actual aphrodisiac.

But I couldn't tell old Fire Helmet that. He wouldn't have believed it. There he sat, leaning forward, peering confidently at me, almost beseechingly, naïvely frank at last, and really, or so I felt, for a Great Bull Buffalo, a little touching in his predicament.

I had to do something, and under stress I had a make-shift inspiration of sorts. My black friends in Haiti were accustomed to concoct a potent and ungodly brew called red-cat to which they attributed, probably wrongly, a tremendous efficacy in such matters. I had seen it concocted and had also drunk some of it, with no memorable effect other than burning my gizzard. But it occurred to me that it couldn't do old Fire Helmet any harm, and might conceivably, with the aid of his imagination, help him.

We had a lot of fun next day procuring and preparing the ingredients. The meat of the big conch shell which the Haitians use was impossible to get in the inland forest, but fresh-water shellfish from the near-by Sassandra were common, and we found some in the village, already dried, which I pounded to powder in a wooden mortar. Then, following the Haitian formula, I pounded up some dry pods of red pepper. We did all this with a certain infantile secrecy in my hut with only Diisi and Fire Helmet present, pop-eyed and curious. By the Haitian recipe you take a bottle of rum two thirds full, add a big handful of powdered dried shellfish, another generous handful of powdered red pepper, cork it, put it in the sun for a day or two, and then if it hasn't exploded you drink it and hope for the best.

In this case, however, if only to stimulate confidence, it seemed necessary to add something mysterious from my medicine box. I thought of permanganate crystals, which make a fine effect, but was afraid they might poison him. I compromised by adding a pinch of effervescent fruit salts, a little cocaine, and two pyramidon tablets.

We hung the bottle by a string in the sun all day, and that evening we tasted it. It was all right. In addition to burning like liquefied brimstone and setting the guts afire, it tasted something awful. Fire Helmet batted his eyes and hurriedly took a long, deep breath. He slapped me on the shoulder and said that it was certainly the stuff he needed. His wrinkled and slightly comical old face beamed with a gratitude which I feared might be somewhat premature. I didn't know whether to feel ashamed of myself or to hope that it might really help him. I had a sort of hope, however, for faith is always a beautiful thing, and a stiff slug of rum alone has been known to put new life into old bones.

Confident and optimistic, Fire Helmet asked for definite directions. I told him to send for a couple of his favorite wives and to take the bottle to bed with them, but for God's sake not to drink more than half of it, whatever happened—that it was an excellent medicament when taken in moderation, but that if he drank all of it in one evening it might kill him. Having already tasted it, he said, he believed me.

Night fell and I was in the hut with the carbide lantern lighted, trying to read Guillaume Apollinaire, but Fire Helmet was on my conscience, and I couldn't keep my attention fixed. Presently I turned off the light, but neither could I go to sleep. Finally toward ten o'clock I went out. The whole village was silent beneath the bright African stars. Fire Helmet's big house across the compound was dark and silent as the grave. I am ashamed to relate that I strolled over to an indiscreet proximity, but heard nothing.

So, praying for the best, I went to bed again. A little later as I was finally dropping off to sleep, I heard, "Pssst! Monsieur!"—somebody arousing me. It was Diisi and Fire Helmet without his fire helmet. The king was slightly tight and so happy that he couldn't wait until morning to tell me the news. I lighted a candle. He was waving his arms and shouting. He was the happiest cannibal king in Africa, and when he had finished bragging and thanking me, I went to sleep in earnest with a considerable weight off my conscience.

Next morning Diisi came to tell me that the chief cook of the tribe had arrived and was over in the yard of Fire Helmet's house, and that he was an old man, and that he was a sorehead, and that he was in a bad humor. Fire Helmet was still asleep. Diisi took me over to introduce us. The cook's name was N'lo. He was a big, flabby, ugly fellow, side-whiskered and short-bearded like an old-fashioned Irishman, partly bald, with a tuft above his forehead. His face was daubed with gray chalk. He wore brass anklets, and suspended from his neck was a big sack made of monkey fur, which Diisi said contained his knives and other culinary tools. He merely grunted that he had come a long, hot distance for nothing, wouldn't talk, seemed definitely to dislike me on first sight, and though he became less surly later I don't think he ever liked me much. I think he kept a special personal dislike for me, but I imagine also that he disliked whites in general, was sorry to see them in his country.

Just now it was useless to question him, for he refused to respond politely even to ordinary questions about his health and family and the weather. Fire Helmet gave him a talking-to later, scolding him and explaining me as best he could, and in the late afternoon there was a palaver with a number of other tribal dignitaries present who flattered the sour old man, made much of him, and persuaded him to promise to answer any questions I cared to ask.

I thought it might be sensible to begin with purely culinary questions which touched directly on his functions as a chef. If N'lo was still somewhat surly, he was interested in his trade; so it went not too badly. Furthermore he was prodded and encouraged by the others, who frequently interpolated comments.

I thus finally obtained a number of specific recipes and other interesting kitchen data from an Ivory Coast cannibal cook who has been practicing his trade for fifty years and occasionally still practices it today.

Here is the Gueré recipe for roast *en brochette:* Cut the meat in good-sized chunks, but let none of the chunks be larger than a leg of sheep. Wash them and sprinkle them with salt. If they are to be put aside before roasting, wrap them in fresh leaves. Remove the leaves, and fix the meat on iron spits or iron hooks above wood embers. Roast very slowly, turning frequently and basting with fresh palm oil, to which you begin adding the ordinary condiments, a little more salt and red pepper only after the meat has roasted for a time. Roast slowly "from late at night until early morning," or "from mid-morning to mid-afternoon." When ready, garnish with ignames, manioc, patates, rice, breadfruit, or bananas (the unsweetened sort for cooking which are only edible when boiled or baked).

The barbecue method—that is, roasting the carcass whole over a pit of coals as the Pacific island cannibals are said to do, and as farmers in Georgia do pigs and sheep—is not practiced, according to N'lo, among his people.

Here is the common recipe for Gueré stew: Cut the meat into pieces the size of your fist and boil in not too much water, with seasoning of salt and whole red pepper pods, "from middle morning until late afternoon." When the stew has simmered down, add quantities of rice boiled separately. N'lo and the others, nodding vigorous assent, insisted that for the stew you must always have rice, that it was not so delicious with bananas or other vegetables, whereas for the roast any vegetable was good.

A dish for royal, rare occasions was a variation of the *foutou*, an Ivory Coast specialty which may be prepared with any sort of meat and which is as famous in the forest as chop suey in Chinatown. It has certain similarities to chop suey. The meat is cut into quite small pieces, parboiled, braised, served on top of rice cooked separately, and over it is poured profusely a highly seasoned hot sauce in which palm oil and peanut oil, thickened with finely pounded roasted peanuts, are mixed in equal quantities. To eat chicken *foutou* even in white surroundings at Dakar, Konakry, or Grand Bassam, is a real gastronomic experience if the black cook sticks to his tradition. It is equally good with pork. It is a dish which, barring the particular sort of meat recommended by N'lo, could make the fortune of a Harlem restaurant. Monkey chitterlings and rice can't touch it.

Another method of preparation, perfectly natural, yet surprising to me, since I had never thought of it in connection with cannibals, was smoked meat. N'lo said that in the old days when there was more freedom, more fighting, and consequently sometimes more good fresh meat than they knew what to do with, it was salted, smoked, and kept, as they do antelope haunches and the big dried catfish.

Returning to the other recipes, I asked what parts of the meat were considered the best. He replied that for solid meat the loin cuts, the ribs, and rump steak were the best. The liver, heart, and brains were tidbits, but tasted identically the same as those of all other animals. Fire Helmet interpolated that as a matter of personal choice, the palm of the hand was the most tender and delicious morsel of all.

There was one point in these recipes which seemed to me somewhat strange, to wit, the unusual length of time they took for cooking. They were all in agreement on the explanation. They said that the meat was the best you could imagine when sufficiently well cooked, but that it was tougher than most and therefore must be cooked longer and more slowly.

"But what about young tender meat?" I asked. "For

instance, a fine plump young girl roasted with bananas. That ought to be tender as any lamb."

They looked at me in some surprise. They all began talking at once, some of them laughing and others indignant. "But we don't eat children and babies," they said. "We are Gueré warriors. Such things have certainly happened, but if you want to know about things like that, go find some woman who was starving, or go and ask some Panther Man in the French prisons." One of the old counselors looked at me gravely and added a simple saying, full of self-respect, and which might stand, I thought, as a motto for their tribe: "We are men, and eaters of men."

These Gueré, then, as nearly as I could understand, were in the traditional anthropological and ethnological sense true cannibals.

I must try to explain carefully what I mean by this distinction. Four wholly different sorts of cannibalism are known to exist, and merging them indiscriminately, as casual commentators have so often done, leads to confusion. They must be clearly separated, for in both motive and practice they are highly differentiated:

Number One. Religious cannibalism. In a group or tribe or nation which does not normally or habitually eat human flesh, there is performed from time to time a human sacrifice, sometimes a man but frequently a young child or virgin, usually around our Easter, and followed by a ritual partaking of the body and blood of the victim.

Number Two. Magical cannibalism. In a group which does not normally eat human flesh, certain of its members, usually those initiated in sorcery, will sometimes eat the brains or heart of one who has been particularly intelligent or particularly brave, with the imitative-magical idea that eating will endow them with similar qualities.

(These religious and magical practices, of course, are as widespread and old as humanity and have by no means been confined exclusively to savages or blacks. Our Christian partaking of the body and blood of the man-god Christ—symbolically among Protestants and literally, it is taught, among Catholics, who believe in transubstantiation—is an interesting civilized survival of more ancient sacrificial rites.)

Number Three. Cannibalism resorted to by isolated starving individuals or groups for the sole sad reason that they cannot procure other food; and cannibalism practiced by individual criminals and monsters as a degenerate by-product of murder.

Number Four. Natural cannibalism. By this I mean the tribe or group which eats human flesh habitually, not from ritual, religious, or magic motives, not because they cannot find other food, and not as a degenerate by-product of crime, but simply because they consider it good meat.

Such I do believe were these Gueré, and how they became traditionally cannibal is a point on which, instead of theorizing, I mean to let them speak here for themselves.

When I said to them, "How is it that you are cannibal while neighboring tribes are not?" their first useless answer, of course, was, "The Gueré have always been cannibal." It was like asking a Georgia farmer why he ate cornbread or a New Englander why he ate white.

But presently in the course of general talk an old counselor hushed the others and said: "We have attacked and fought a certain village. We have slain some men there with our spears. We have marched a long way, we have fought well, we are hungry, and we want to feast. Perhaps there are sheep and goats and chickens in the conquered village, perhaps not, but why slay them when there is already slain provision of good meat? Is it reasonable to let it spoil and wastefully kill other which is no better? You have asked *us* many questions and we have answered."

They waited now to hear what I had to say. Decidedly this black old Socrates had passed the buck. As he had framed his query, no criminal element of murder was involved. True, they had killed some human neighbors in a fight. But who was I, or any white man, in the name of Julius Caesar, Charlemagne, Saint Louis and the Cru-

saders of the Lord, U. S. Grant and Sherman, Luden-
dorff and Papa Joffre and Sergeant York, to tell black
Socrates that it was all right for us to do it with machine
guns, poison gas, and bombs, but naughty-naughty and
uncivilized for him to do it with a spear?

"The reason, my dear unenlightened friends, why you
shouldn't eat your neighbors is because you shouldn't
have killed them in the first place!"

If one isn't a Methodist missionary, one must preserve
a shred of intellectual decency at least, even in a discussion with cannibals. Decidedly, that answer was out.
And being out, just what did it leave for our further
philosophic and moral consideration? It left the flesh of
the mammal *homo sapiens*, not criminally murdered, no
longer *sapiens* since he was dead, freshly, cleanly killed,
and according to their statement, yet to be verified, excellent meat. To my asking why they ate it, they had turned
the question back against me, saying, "Why shouldn't
we eat it?"

I ask my gentle readers not to become impatient at this
point for fear I am going to advocate roast German with
sauerkraut *à la* Bernard Shaw or grilled Japanese on
toast as a supplement to our next Hooverized war menus
—though the rice-fed Japanese might be more tender
and tasty than most.

There is a very special and sufficient reason, I think,

why cannibalism is not for us. But the point here involved with my black Socrates was why, if for any reason, cannibalism was not for him.

Biologically cannibalism is a widely general though not universal practice, and consequently "natural" in the purely scientific sense. Insects devour insects, fish devour fish, mammals devour mammals. We civilized human mammals devour our four-footed cousins large and small. But we do not eat the biped Arthur Jones. The reason we refrain from eating him is partly, of course, simply that we are unaccustomed to the idea. But we have also, I think, a deeper, more honest, and more defensible reason. We believe that in the essence of a man there is something holy which other animals have not—to wit, a soul. The body is its temple, we say, and even after the soul has fled we feel, sentimentally at least, that the carcass is still sacred. This feeling, even if founded ultimately on pure sentiment alone, is a sound and sufficient reason for refraining. A sentimental qualm is as logical and defensible a reason as any for not doing a thing.

But this reason—good and sufficient for us—would have made no sense whatever in a discussion with the Gueré. They too believe that man has a soul. But they believe with equal conviction that everything has a soul (not only all other animals but also the banana plant, the potato vine, the vegetable, the grain of rice), so that if they considered that the anterior possession of a soul made a material body subsequently inedible, *they would immediately starve to death.* They believe, like the saintly poet William Blake, that "everything that lives is holy." But when the vital spark goes out they deem that the holiness has betaken itself elsewhere, and that if what remains is good to eat, it may be eaten with clear conscience and healthy appetite.

So it was, therefore, that caught socratically in this interesting discussion with Fire Helmet, his counselors and cook, I was compelled to say finally, "I can't seem to think of any reason why you others shouldn't eat it if you like it." And I added, "As a matter of fact, I should like very much to try it myself, just once."

III

ONE morning runners, guides, and porters—savage fellows bristling with spears—came down from the north with gifts and an invitation from the old king Gedao, whose name meant the Torch, and whom I had promised to visit in his village on some fine future day.

The gifts were royal—haunches of dried meat, great packets of pink kola in palm leaves bound with withes. The invitation was equally generous, and pressing. Gedao, I suspected, having heard rumors of high jinks, feasting and dancing, tin trunks full of handsome necklaces, mirrors, good steel horn-handled knives and what not, bottles of wine that bubbled—I can never thank Paul Morand enough for having said, "Don't go into Africa, my friend, with empty hands and don't carry only ten-cent-store trash unless you expect to bring out trashy impressions in return"—Gedao, I was amiably inclined to think, had become perhaps a little worried over my prolonged stay in a friendly rival's territory, and wanted to share in the fun.

This seemed reasonable enough, and the messengers said that if I did come Gedao was planning to put on a series of war games for my entertainment. It was a three days' journey and wouldn't be easy, but I decided to make it. Fire Helmet even considered coming along, but was dissuaded on my promise that I would visit him again before leaving the country.

The runners had gone before us, and Gedao met us on the outskirts of Blo-di, his capital, his braided hair still porcupined with polished bone and ivory sticks, accompanied by a knot of notables. But his greeting, though effusive, was embarrassed, and as we entered the big village it was evident that something unnatural was going on, for all the hut doors were closed, and not a woman, child, or baby was in sight, nor any of the usual dancers and shouters of welcome.

He explained apologetically that one of the devil-maskers, accoutered precisely to take part in the welcoming ceremonies, had gone on a rampage of his own, had torn down a house, had broken the arm of one of his acolytes, had cracked a number of heads, though not fatally, and was still on the loose. He couldn't be interfered with, they told me, for when a masker of this category runs amuck, it is a sign that a real devil, a real *Gla*, has incarnated itself in the body which wears the mask, and is out to inflict ritual chastisement. One must placate him, or keep out of his way, or accept his buffeting without retaliation, until the frenzy has passed.

From a distant part of the village we heard shouting, but could see nothing of what was occurring. Gedao led us through the deserted streets and into the private fenced compound of the hut which had been reserved for me. With a demon running wild, he said, there was nothing to do but make the best of it and postpone the dances, pantomimes, and *griot* songs for the morrow. Meanwhile he helped superintend my installation. There were clean straw mats and panther skins to loll and sleep on, big earthen pots of water, a calabash of banghi, a thick, polished hand-hewn board set on stakes for a table, mortars for pounding grain upturned to serve as chairs. After the simplifications Wamba had taught me in ambulant housekeeping, most of my elaborate and expensive "explorer's" equipment, except for a filter, a mosquito net, and a carbide lantern, had been left, thank God, behind.

Gedao advised both Diisi and me to rest indoors until the hullabaloo grew calmer. He couldn't understand that a fortuitous event like the presence of a demon might interest me more—at a safe distance—than any of the planned formal entertainment. In Haiti I had once seen a god incarnate, but I had never met a devil face to face in flesh and blood, not even a masked one, and I was all for having a respectful look, if possible, at this fellow.

So, led by Gedao, we cautiously approached the part of the village where Gla was still rampaging. There were crowds there, men only, but a good many of them, ready to scatter and run, keeping their distance, yet pushing forward as much as they dared, like a crowd at home attracted by an interesting but dangerous wild beast that had escaped from a menagerie cage, each individual hoping perhaps that somebody else might get bitten, but prepared to take to his heels if the beast singled him out to chase.

It was almost, indeed, as if they were baiting the devil and encouraging him. He wore a hideous mask, gorilla-featured, three times larger than a human face, festooned with bones and teeth and bells, and in the gaping mouth were set ugly, shining metal fangs which increased the expression of grotesque ferocity. The mask formed part of a heavy hood covering completely head and shoulders, with metal-clawed mittens covering his hands, and he wore also a flaring long grass skirt. Hampered by all that weight, he didn't seem to me really very dangerous, rushing awkwardly this way and that, as if he were getting tired and couldn't see very well through the eye-slits in the mask. But he brandished a heavy staff and from time to time hurled it savagely into the dodging crowd. Scared acolytes had to retrieve it and return it to him, and if they didn't dodge away sharply enough, risked a whack over their shoulders for their pains. It was thus, they said, he had broken a young man's arm in his first frenzy, and they insisted impressively that Gla was the Great Chastiser, but it was evident that I had come too late for any real excitement. What I actually saw was not much more impressive than any rough, awkward game. He staggered over toward a hut and tore at the thatching, and then as if unable to keep his attention fixed on any one attack, rushed into the crowd, raining harmless awkward blows at random. With each new rush he staggered more and presently flopped down like a mechanical doll in a ballet.

We gathered close, waiting to see whether the paroxysm was really over, and soon from inside the mask came a very tired human voice, grumbling and complaining. It must have been extremely wearing to be possessed by so rampageous a devil, and it must have been terribly hot inside all that heavy costume. They lifted him up like a sick man, holding him by the arms, and led him stumbling away.

Next morning occurred the formal reception which this devil business had delayed. There is a certain social etiquette and formality in the forest just as in the salons of Paris and the apartments of Park Avenue. So I was presented now to Gedao somewhat as another visiting chief might have been, and as if we had not intimately met before.

I sat in front of my hut with Diisi, and Gedao came in procession with his counselors and entertainers while the whole village gathered round to watch the ceremonial. After the presentation Gedao and I sat side by side, holding hands like a couple of sweethearts. His chief *griot* pointed to us both, shouting, gesticulating, shaking his finger in our faces, pointing us out to the crowd, and demanding silence. Then addressing Gedao, he sang:

> *The Gueré are always the strongest,*
> *But he is the strongest of all.*
> *Among the warriors he is king;*
> *He leads and gives good counsel.*
> *If he is killed, we are all lost.*

Gedao arose and responded:

"Yes, what he says is true. If I am killed, you are all lost. I am a hawk in the eye of the sun."

When the tumult of hurrahs had ceased, the *griot* turned to me and sang:

> *He is a great chief who comes alone,*
> *Without white followers*
> *And company of men in uniform.*

JUNGLE WAYS

Behold how he has come!
He has come in friendship as a brother,
And he has come bearing gifts.

They were frankly keen, like children, about the gifts, and kept pointing to the tin trunk with eager curiosity. It is nice to be welcomed for oneself alone, but when people come from far away we all enjoy seeing them fish out little surprises from their baggage. However, among these generous people, I was to receive gifts as well as give them. Gedao presented me with a handsome crocodile-hide amulet and a pair of hippo teeth as beautiful as ivory, leather-mounted, hung on a braided necklace. I gave him a hunting-knife with belt and sheath, a brightly colored smock, and some bottles of sweet sparkling wine. For the *griot* there was a large pair of scissors which he promptly hung around his neck from a leather string. A procession of servants brought food in calabashes—a sheep's liver, live chickens, kola nuts, rice, eggs, dried fish, etc. I must examine each dish as it passed and exclaim how good it looked. In turn I presented Gedao, for the village, with thirty pounds of bar salt, and there was glad shouting.

My tin treasure chest was opened, containing trivial minor gifts for all the entertainers, and the fun began in earnest. Since the men were to do the big war game

176

later, the present stars were mostly girls and women, singly or in groups, who sang, danced, and pantomimed. It was like a Sunday school Christmas tree night at a Salvation Army celebration in the Bowery. Each received a necklace or a box of beads, a bottle of perfumery, a tin of talcum powder, a mirror, or some other shining trifle.

Most of them were delighted, but every so often toward the end of it a girl's face would fall when she received her little gift, and she would seem on the verge of bursting into tears. Her sister, perhaps, had received a mirror, and she wanted a mirror too instead of the necklace or beads I offered. Where possible I rectified these errors, and thought how human we all are, even the dancing daughters of the unspoiled cannibals.

The best of them all was a muscular young woman with a cloth draped skirtlike round her loins who leaped into the ring on all fours, growling, grimacing, chattering, and pretending to bite at the legs of the crowd, which drew back with mock fear and cried, "What is it? Is it a woman, or is it a big ape?" Some said, "Don't be afraid, it's only a woman." Others cried, "No, take care!" Other dancing girls now began to bait her, prodding her with sticks, and running back into the crowd, shrieking and laughing as she chased them on all fours, biting the legs of some, still growling and chattering. Finally they tore her skirt off and shouted, "See! See!" She had a long monkey tail, a real monkey tail, fur tuft and all, fastened in its proper place with leather strings. As she grimaced and leaped in marvelous pantomime, pretending now to try to escape, they all shouted, "Yes, it is indeed a big ape!" This was the measure of her artistic triumph; Diisi explained that when the crowd is dissatisfied with this particular pantomime, they point to the strings after the skirt is torn off and cry, "Bah, look, it's only a woman masquerading." Jungle cabaret. Source stuff for *Blackbirds* and Josephine Baker.

In the war games which were to take place in the afternoon Gedao explained that they would proceed as if going forth to actual battle and that he himself would lead the warriors. Toward two o'clock the war drums were set booming. All the men and initiated youths of the village came, more than a hundred of them, augmented soon by arriving groups from other villages. They congregated quietly. The only noise just now was the booming of the drums. They came armed with spears, assegais, swords, machetes, war-clubs. When they had congregated to the number of about two hundred, they quit the village, still quietly, disappearing into the forest. I would have given a great deal to witness the preparation they were undergoing, since part of it was secret-society ritual, but in these matters one had to be locally initiate—a long process beginning with puberty, and in certain matters even before birth. There are many things in the forest which no white, however intimate, or however willing to obey the Fetich code, will ever see. Thanks partly to preliminary initiations undergone in Haiti, and partly to the opening of certain barriers in Africa by Wamba and her associates, I have seen more than the casual traveler, but the more one learns, the more one realizes how little he has learned, and I know that all that I have ever seen is nothing, for that which is hidden is hidden and will never be revealed.

So Diisi and I, with a few feeble old grandfathers, sat twiddling our thumbs in the deserted village. The women and children had all been sent indoors. The drums had ceased, and everything was silence.

Then finally out of the silent greenness of the thick forest edge they came. It was as if a gigantic legendary serpent were emerging, for they came single file, bent forward at the waist, their painted bodies touching. The serpent's head was Gedao, his body painted a dull red, his face smeared black with charcoal grease, a sword in his right hand, a club in his left, and a piece of panther skin fastened with a chain across his shoulders. They came stealthily without a sound, and wound stealthily into the village, a long, living, gigantic multicolored serpent, bristling with spears. Their bodies were painted with pig-mented clay of various colors in swirls Picasso-like, monstrous pythonlike, but all their faces were smeared dead black, and each man held between his teeth a green leaf.

Arriving in the central clearing, they wound spirally, bending low to earth with lowered spears, all this in silence still. A shrill whistle sounded and pandemonium broke loose. The serpent broke up into a wild disorder of leaping, howling warriors, grimacing madly, brandishing their weapons, crouching and leaping, imitating all the gesture of actual battle. The women now appeared at the hut doors, shrieking encouragement. Out of the disorder emerged presently an almost equally wild formalized dance done in circling procession as the American redskins used to do, to the sound of the drums which had again begun booming.

There was a somewhat terrifying reality about it, as if they were being carried away by the game and doing it now in deadly earnest. The women shrieked and wept, and an old blind man, groveling on his knees, screaming, seizing hold of people's feet and pointing to his sightless eyes, begged to be protected from the killers.

But it was, after all, only a superb wild mimicry. A new era had come with the French, and not even the Gueré dared any longer make war openly on their neighbors. There were still occasional small raids, usually in remote territory, plotted and carried out with utmost secrecy, and always with the risk of afterward being punished. And each year they were becoming more and more rare.

All this was reflected in certain of the songs which Diisi translated for me. I was in the presence, for good or bad as one may choose to see it, of a dying tradition—a thing always tinged, apart from the most reasonable moral and utilitarian considerations, with a certain underlying sadness. For these changes, however necessary, are taking a certain brave, kaleidoscopic color out of life. In another hundred or another thousand years, we may all work in offices and factories, eat and dress and think alike, love our neighbors as ourselves (since we will have no neighbors anywhere on the globe who have not been either exterminated or transformed into our own image), ride in Fords, and be at peace. It will be a good thing for the sheep, for the flock, but the tiger burning bright needs no millennium. The world will perhaps be better and safer, but it will be less beautiful when all the bright tigers are dead or shut up in cages. I am not decrying "world betterment" or "the march of civilization" on any intelligent or logical grounds. I am just begging leave to be a little sad about it, reflecting for a moment the sadness of this tiny, unimportant, doomed sav-

181

age tribe, which came out so poignantly and curiously in their songs.

This is the song that the Gueré youths sang, those who had been recently initiated into the war dances:

> *Our fathers were men.*
> *Now we do as they taught us.*
> *We follow their steps*
> *And shout as they do—*
> *So as not to forget.*

And this is the song made by a nameless warrior who was growing old:

To be a chief in battle
You must be proud and brave.
My body bears many scars,
For I was both.
Once I was proud and brave among the spears.
Now they say I must do what the white man tells me.

In the twilight, when it was all over, after quiet had been restored in the village, I sat talking with Gedao about these and many things. It was a time for confidences, and for true words.

He said: "Alas, this has been a good day, but not like the old days. We have danced the dance of warriors, we have shouted bravely, but I know that I will never again lead my tribe in force to battle. It is too strong for us. We all know it. We are slowly becoming women. But we can never forget that we once were men."

Indeed they were still men, these Gueré, and I told him so, the finest I had met in the forest. And I was glad that I had come among them before the old tradition had completely died.

IV

THE occasion was one which would probably never be repeated, so that I felt in duty bound to make the most of it. In addition, therefore, to a portion of stew with rice, sure to be so highly seasoned with red pepper that fine shades of flavor might be lost to an unaccustomed palate, I had requested and been given a sizable rump steak, also a small loin roast to cook or have cooked in whatever manner I pleased.

It was the meat of a freshly killed man, who seemed to be about thirty years old—and who had not been murdered.

Neither then nor at any time since have I had any serious personal qualms, either of digestion or conscience, but despite time, distance, and locale, I feel that it would be unfair, unsporting, and ungrateful to involve and identify too closely the individual friends who made my experience possible.

Fortunately such identification will not be necessary to establish authenticity. When a man has actually done a special thing of this sort, he need never worry about

184

whether it will be accepted as authentic. Some millions of people will sooner or later read these lines in one language or another. No matter what phrases I choose, whether I write well or awkwardly, the authenticity will take care of itself, for I propose to set down details as full, objective, and complete as if I were recounting a first experience with reindeer meat, shark meat, or any other unfamiliar meat experimented with for the first time.

The raw meat, in appearance, was firm, slightly coarse-textured rather than smooth. In raw texture, both to the eye and to the touch, it resembled good beef. In color, however, it was slightly less red than beef. But it was reddish. It was not pinkish or grayish like mutton or pork. Through the red lean ran fine whitish fibers, interlacing, seeming to be stringy rather than fatty, suggesting that it might be tough. The solid fat was faintly yellow, as the fat of beef and mutton is. This yellow tinge was very faint, but it was not clear white as pork fat is.

In smell it had what I can only describe as the familiar, characteristic smell of any good fresh meat of the larger domestic animals. I am not expert in the finest shades of odor. When various meats begin cooking, there are special odors, easily distinguishable once they begin sizzling, as for instance beef, mutton, and pork. But in the raw state meats even so different as the three I have mentioned smell exactly alike to me, and this present meat smelled the same.

Having at hand my portion of highly seasoned stew, prepared in the classic manner (and not yet tasted because I was anxious to get the clearest first impression possible of the natural meat, and feared that excessive condiments would render it inconclusive), I had determined to prepare the steak and roast in the simplest manner, as nearly as possible as we prepare meat at home. The small roast was spitted, since an oven was out of the question, and after it had been cooking for a while I set about grilling the steak. I tried to do it exactly as we do at home. It took longer, but that may have been partly because of the difference between gas flame and wood coals.

The cooking odors, wholly pleasant, were like those of beefsteak and roast beef, with no special other distinguishing odor. By "other distinguishing odor," I mean that if you go into a kitchen where they are cooking game or mutton or fish or chicken, there is in each case something quite special which you can distinguish with the nose alone.

When the roast began to brown and the steak to turn blackish on the outside, I cut into them to have a look at the partially cooked interior. It had turned quite definitely paler than beef would turn. It was turning grayish

186

as veal or lamb would, rather than dark reddish as a beef-steak turns. The fat was sizzling, becoming tender and yellower. Beyond what I have told, there was nothing special or unusual. It was nearly done and it looked and smelled good to eat.

It would have been obviously stupid to go to all this trouble and then taste too meticulously and with too much experimental nervousness only tiny morsels. I had cooked it as one would any other meat for my regular evening dinner, and I proposed to make a meal of it as one would any other meat, with rice and a bottle of wine. That seemed to be the way to do it. I wanted to be absolutely sure of my impressions.

I sat down to it with my bottle of wine, a bowl of rice, salt and pepper at hand. I had thought about this and planned it for a long time, and now I was going to do it. I was going to do it, furthermore—I had promised and told myself—with a completely casual, open, and objective mind. But I was soon to discover that I had bluffed and deceived myself a little in pretending so detached an attitude. It was with, or rather after, the first mouthful, that I discovered there had been unconscious bravado in me, a small bluff-hidden unconscious dread. For my first despicable reaction—so strong that it took complete precedence over any satisfaction or any fine points of gastronomic shading—was simply a feeling of thankful and immense relief. At any rate, it was perfectly good to eat! At any rate, it had no weird, startling, or unholy special flavor. It was good to eat, and despite all the intelligent, academic detachment with which I had thought I was approaching the experience, my poor little, cowardly and prejudiced subconscious real self sighed with relief and patted itself on the back.

I took a good big swallow of wine, a helping of rice, and thoughtfully ate half the steak. And as I ate, I knew with increasing conviction and certainty exactly what it was like. It was like good, fully developed veal, not young, but not yet beef. It was very definitely like that, and it was not like any other meat I had ever tasted. It was so nearly like good, fully developed veal that I think no person with a palate of ordinary, normal sensitiveness could distinguish it from veal. It was a mild, good meat with no other sharply defined or highly characteristic taste such as for instance goat, high game, and pork have. The steak was slightly tougher than prime veal, a little stringy, but not too tough or stringy to be agreeably edible. The roast, from which I cut and ate a central slice, was tender, and in color, texture, smell as well as taste, strengthened my certainty that of all the meats we habitually know, veal is the one meat to which this meat is accurately comparable. As for any other special taste or odor of a sort which would be surprising

and make a person who had tasted it not knowing exclaim, "What is this?" it had absolutely none. And as for
the "long pig" legend, repeated in a thousand stories and
recopied in a hundred books, it was totally, completely
false. It gives me great comfort here to be able to write
thus categorically. A small helping of the stew might
likewise have been veal stew, but the overabundance of
red pepper was such that it conveyed no fine shading to a
white palate; so I was glad I had tried it first in the simpler ways.

If I had begun, despite my objective intentions, with a
certain unconscious trepidation, I finished well enough,
able after the first sensation of relief had passed to consider the meat as meat, and to be absolutely sure of the
correctness of my impressions. And I felt a great satisfaction in having learned the empiric truth on a subject concerning which far too many books and pieces have been
written and rewritten, filled with almost nothing but
speculation, hearsay, legend, and hot air. A sense of pride
also in having carried something through to its finish.
And a long-standing personal curiosity satisfied at last.

PART THREE
TIMBUCTOO INTERLUDE

I

THE Moro Naba, King of all the Mossi, the one great black potentate still ruling in West Central Africa, whom we had detoured some hundred miles to see, having said good-by to our friends on the Ivory Coast and now motor-trucking up toward Timbuctoo, sat on his throne in robes of purple and gold at Ouagadougou in the High Volta and was politely bored.

Katie and I sat on two small wooden chairs placed facing the throne about ten feet back from it, with our eyes on a level with his enormous stomach, and were also beginning to be politely bored.

So finally to give the interview some point, if only that of being thrown out of the palace, I asked as innocently as possible, "Is it true, Your Majesty, what they say, that if you ever look upon the face of your cousin, the Yatanga Naba, one of you will die before the coming of the new moon?"

He grunted, startled, astonished rather than angry, leaned forward, and demanded, "Who told you that?"

From this point on, the audience was not boring. The

trouble had been that the French governor who had arranged it had instructed us too carefully how to comport ourselves, what compliments to offer, what questions were polite and safe. So I had been saying how honored we were to be there, or something just as dumb, and up to now the increasing mutual boredom had only been relieved by the fact that every time the king replied how honored he was that we should be there, or something even dumber, his thirty male concubines who lay or crouched round the foot of his throne in lascivious motion picture attitudes, naked and covered with bracelets and jewels like women, would snap their fingers in unison, strike up their lutes, shiver, buzz cooingly like wounded doves for an instant, and then resume their sculptural silence.

It was the same when the king broke wind, which he did rather loudly and frequently. The Moro Naba rules in a direct dynastic line from the early sixteenth century, and dynastic kings enjoy social prerogatives denied to upstart presidents and Mussolini. For that matter, these rumbling interruptions were no more empty than the words we had been speaking. If I could have replied at will in kind, the audience would have been perfect. It was only the talk which had been boring. What we were seeing would have caused the average Hollywood director to commit suicide.

TIMBUCTOO INTERLUDE

The Moro Naba, black as ink, with heavy tattooed jowls and almost as wide at the girth as he was tall, sat among his concubines cloaked in robes of purple velvet elaborately embroidered in gold, with velvet boots also gold-embroidered, and a gold-encrusted skull cap. He lived in luxury on generous French appointments, in this Moorish-looking palace on the edge of Ouagadougou, finer than the governor's, and was allowed to keep all the gilded and savage state of the Moro Nabas who had ruled before him—on condition, naturally, that he would "cooperate" with his French advisers in matters which were economic or political. The most extraordinary of these traditional survivals was the male harem posturing there, flung round on the throne's platform, at his feet. It is the only harem of its special kind, I think, which exists openly anywhere in the world today. They were black youths ranging in age from around sixteen to twenty-one, whose hair had been let grow long, arranged fantastically in female fashion, whose eyes were painted, whose gestures were effeminate, and who conducted themselves exactly as would the slaves of a female seraglio. From time to time, with hand or cheek, they would fawn against the feet of the Moro Naba, looking impudently with their made-up eyes at Katie and me the while. Some of them were rather beautiful in their perverse, hermaphroditic way.

Even in the heart of Africa, or perhaps because it was in Africa, this harem seemed a strange anomaly, for homosexuality is extremely rare among primitive Negroes, and the Mossi were a savage, primitive, Fetich-worshiping warrior people, pure-blood black. But there was a special explanation for it. In surrounding himself with boys, the Moro Naba was following a hereditary and obligatory tradition of the Mossi kings, independent perhaps of any original natural personal inclination, for he also had wives and begot children by them as his forebears necessarily had likewise done.

The tradition of this custom in the royal family dates from the early seventeenth century, when one of the great warrior Moro Nabas was gone six months to the wars against the Moslems who had come down from the north, in a rapidly moving cavalry campaign where neither wife nor woman could follow. He had, however, among his personal attendants a devoted young boy slave who was his body servant. This boy cooked for him, helped him dress, mended his clothes, in fact performed every domestic service that women had performed for him at home. So that one day the Moro Naba said to himself, "He already does everything for me that a woman can, except one thing—why not that also?" And according to the history, which involved a triumphal campaign, every succeeding Moro Naba, in unbroken royal line from that time on, has had youths in his harem.

There was another curious custom which dated from those martial days of Mossi glory. The only time the present Moro Naba ever went actually to war was in 1914 when he raised and led four thousand mounted Mossi volunteers for African duty under French colors—but every morning toward eight o'clock, every day in the year, now as in the old days, the Moro Naba must rush out on the terrace of his palace shouting, "Bring me my horse!" as Porgy shouts in the theater, "Bring me my goat!"

Amid tumult and shouting, the war horse is brought, magnificently caparisoned, and the Moro Naba, who weighs nigh three hundred pounds, demands a ladder to mount it and ride out to war and slaughter. At this moment his ministers rush about him to dissuade him. He berates them for their cowardice but finally, unlike Porgy, allows himself to be persuaded to start only on the morrow. He reënters the palace exhausted, still berating his cowardly ministers, and if there are no audiences solaces himself with vermouth, his favorite mild intoxicant. I am told that he can drink twelve bottles at a sitting without wabbling or losing his royal dignity. Gossip in Ouagadougou says that the Moro Naba is mildly drunk all the time, like the squire in *Tom Jones*, and has been so without interruption for the past twenty years, that he has

197

become lazy, fat, and spoiled, a puppet sunken in debauchery.

At the beginning of our audience he had seemed, indeed, a bit vague and lethargic, but when I fired the innocently indiscreet and point-blank question about his cousin, the Yatanga Naba, he awoke with a grunt and displayed what seemed to me a suspiciously alert intelligence. The Yatanga Naba was by way of being a bit of a thorn in the flesh of the Moro Naba. While the Moro was king of all the Mossi, the Yatanga was a sort of pope, who lived in another palace on equally generous French appointments, in Ouiagouia, not very far away, and who exercised also temporal powers in a limited district. The Mossi themselves say that while the Moro is legitimately king, the old Yatanga possesses, hidden somewhere in his palace, the ancient Fetich of the Mossi tribes, and that through possessing it he remains the spiritual leader of the kingdom. The superstition, or whatever it might be, that if the two ever looked on each other's faces one of them would die, was a general Mossi belief that I had picked up in the Yatanga's territory.

So when the Moro now grunted, "Who told you that? Why do you ask me that?" I replied truthfully that it was a thing said by all the Mossi, that if I understood correctly it seemed to be a matter of magic rather than of politics or plotting, and that since I was interested in matters concerning magic and totally innocent of any purpose or knowledge that touched political or government affairs, I had ventured to ask him about it.

He said, "But who exactly told you? Did anybody pay you to ask me?"

I said, "On my word of honor, no. And if asking you was wrong I will forget that I have asked it. I asked the Yatanga, you know. . . ."

"So, you saw the Yatanga?" he demanded suspiciously, "you have been at Ouiagouia? You asked *him* that? What did *he* say?"

"He said respectfully, Your Majesty, that he had never looked upon your face, and that he surely never would look upon it, and that therefore he would never know whether it was true or not and consequently couldn't tell me."

I don't know what answer the Moro might have been expecting, but at this his suspicious face gradually relaxed, he broke into a guffaw of unroyal negro laughter and said, "Bring your chair a little closer."

He began by asking me all sorts of questions about the Yatanga Naba, boastful little-boy questions, what sort of palace he lived in and whether it wasn't true that it was much less splendid than his own, how many ministers he had, what his horse was like, whether he used a ladder to get on it, what sort of robes he wore?

I answered as honestly and with as much detail as I could, but watching myself carefully, not to say anything that would offend the Moro's vanity, for as a matter of fact the Yatanga in his different way had impressed me as more of a man than the Moro. The Yatanga, whom I had visited hurriedly but less formally with Monsieur Courtot, the French administrator at Ouiagouia, was a giant who topped my six feet by a full head in height, in a bright red cap, pure white robes, a man of bearded and dignified visage, and who, whereas the Moro in his gold and purple wore no savage tribal amulets, had round his neck an amulet of lion claws, a number of ancient leather sorcerer's bags, and on his fingers thick, enormous silver rings that must have weighed each at least a half a pound. He was a giant who could wear them. Among the lion claws and tribal *grigris* which adorned his breast, the red ribbon and enameled cross of the Legion of Honor seemed gratuitous and almost petty.

The Yatanga's palace, in the open courtyard of which he had received us, was a big mud structure, in truth not nearly so fine as the Moro's, but the phallic cones which topped its façade were streaked with the dry blood of beasts recently sacrificed, and instead of an androgyne harem he was surrounded by shaven-headed ministers, also white-robed, who looked like Thibetan priests. The Yatanga, Courtot told me, was an enormous drinker like

200

the king his cousin, but the actual impression I had of him was that of being received by the high priest of a monastery with mysteries within its walls which neither I nor Monsieur Courtot would ever penetrate.

I told the Moro all I could of this, in mitigated form, of how his cousin sat on a big leather cushion instead of a throne, wore no gold embroidery, but seemed occupied with spiritual rather than temporal affairs, and agreed that the palace could in no way be compared to his own magnificent edifice. I added that the Yatanga's only music was a single one-stringed instrument and a man who went before him beating a drum. In short I gave him all the intimate details I could, but took care contemptibly to twist them so that they would flatter the Moro. When the audience ended, he thanked us and said he was glad we had come.

During our whole visit, and including all this latter talk, at each pause after a question of the Moro's—and before I was supposed to reply—the dovelike reclining youths snapped their fingers, twanged their lutes, moaned, and writhed like dying birds or female cats in heat. Katie, who has been to Harlem drags and every dive in the Rue de Lappe, as who has not, was for once absolutely pop-eyed. We agreed that it was well worth having turned aside a hundred miles to see.

II

WITH two vague black boys, one to guide us and one to beat the donkeys, we seemed to be lost in an orchard of thorn trees, planted in the sand and inhabited exclusively by howling jackals. It was around ten o'clock on a black, dinnerless Christmas night, and somewhere, probably only a couple of hundred yards away, was Timbuctoo.

Yao, alias "the colonel," my usually resourceful chauffeur who in most emergencies took command of us and everything, knew all about cars and the forest, but nothing about deserts and donkeys. He looked upon both with disfavor, and refused even to offer advice. He was sore because we had left the truck at Mopti, sore because he had caught lice on the river boat, and sorest of all because I had refused to let him shoot a camel. Katie was sore for reasons of her own, and we were all sore because we were hungry.

Our guides, village boys from the Niger river-landing which we had left only that same afternoon, were afraid to go on in the darkness for fear we might leave Timbuctoo too far on the right or left and go wandering out into the real Sahara. They were all for our waiting ignominiously and supperless until the dawn.

A bored French corporal in slippers and dirty flannel pajamas, with moustaches like a walrus and an American farm lantern, came and rescued us. He had heard our arguments and the braying of our miserable beasts. We were as close as that, and felt very foolish. He led us over a sand dune, skirting dark low walls which had looked to us like nothing but further sand dunes, to an enormous dark rectangular building which might have been an abandoned garrison or palace. It was the ancient caravanserai—on the outskirts of the dead-black city in which not a single light was showing anywhere—with empty rooms to house a hundred guests. Its sole caretaker, an old black Mohammedan named Boubekar, was aroused with difficulty, grumbling, rubbing his sleepy eyes, but once awake and seeing Katie tired, he turned fatherly, kicked his yapping dog, found candles, led us through corridors swarming with bats to a vast clay-walled chamber, also bat-infested but otherwise clean, in which there were beds and a table. In a few minutes he returned with bread and milk and a chicken; so we had a sort of belated Christmas dinner after all, and flung ourselves on the bed and went to sleep without undressing. . . .

We awoke late next morning to look out from our window on what remained of Timbuctoo the mysterious, capital of a once great Negro empire, sprawling there over the sand dunes, jumbled walls of sun-baked clay, yellow and seemingly desolate in the glaring sunlight.

Our caravanserai, dating from the days when no wayfaring stranger could enter the city after dark, was isolated, set back a good two hundred yards from the agglomeration yonder, so that our view had the advantage of perspective. It seemed to be a much bigger place than accounts of recent travelers had led us to expect, for writers generally in recent years have fallen somewhat into the habit of enlarging on the ancient glories of the once great caravan metropolis, and of describing what remains today, perhaps for literary contrast's sake, as desolate and disappointing.

It looked indeed desolate, almost forbidding in the harsh morning glare, for here and there clay roofs were caved in, clay walls crumbled, and there were no signs of animation—but what remained architecturally seemed a compact, big city, many thousands of flat-roofed houses, crowded together, heavy-walled, most of them one-storied with roof terraces, but many of them two stories, and some of them even three stories high.

In our foreground at the left, on the old city's edge,

was a French fort, also clay, and a small parade ground around which were pink-washed buildings which would doubtless be government houses, for the entire administration at Timbuctoo was military. As the caravanserai in which we lodged belonged to the administration, I sent Boubekar across to the government house after breakfast with a card, presenting our thanks for shelter, etc., to the adjutant in charge, or whoever he might find there. An orderly came presently and escorted me to the office of the commandant, a spruce, clean-shaven, easy-mannered Parisian seated at a big flat-topped desk, wearing a civilian sport shirt, flannel trousers, and sandals. His name was Fourré, his family back home lived in an old house in the Rue de Renne, near the Luxembourg Gardens, and he seemed a suave and charming gentleman, as he indeed turned out to be; but I had some slight difficulty in getting my attention focused, for on entering the door of the office I had observed nailed to it conspicuously a pair of human ears which had evidently been quite recently removed from the head of their owner. Since the ears were obviously nailed there to be seen by all, like a sign or a mail-box, I mentioned them. Colonel Fourré said they belonged, or had belonged until the last week, to a particularly unregenerate Tuareg bandit chief who had been robbing and murdering people on the caravan route from Araouan, making trouble for a long time, boasting that he could never be caught, inciting others to make trouble. To kill him would have left him a hero in the eyes of his followers; so they had caught him and cut off his ears —a lesson which, the colonel sententiously remarked, he and all his tribesmen would remember longer than if they had hanged him. Most of the Tuaregs around Timbuctoo, he said, naturally a wicked and troublesome lot, had been gradually tamed and now cultivated their flocks like any other nomads, coming and going freely in the city, trading in the markets and bazaars. There was still a great deal of general trading, he said, despite the fact that the immense caravans of former years no longer came. The average caravan before the war often arrived with as many as 20,000 camels. There was nothing like that any more, but caravans of what he called "average size" still arrived from time to time. He looked for his notes on the last one. It had been a caravan of 2,534 camels from Araouan bringing 10,356 bars of salt weighing 60 kilos (about 120 pounds) each.

The commandant was amiably disposed and apparently not busy for the moment; so I asked him a number of other questions. It had occurred to me that since Timbuctoo remains in poetry and romance—despite the conquest of the Sahara by motor cars and airplanes—one of the few far, remote dream cities of the world like Baghdad of old and Samarkand the Golden, it might be interesting to bring back some specific facts about it in addition to personal comments and impressions.

He averaged the present population of Timbuctoo at 85,000, of which he said only about 15,000 were permanent hereditary householders, lifelong Negro Moslem residents who have owned the old city from generation to generation. The remaining population, he said, might be designated by the paradoxical term of "resident nomad," since they were a floating mixture of all the North African races, both Negro and Arab, who came to the metropolis which linked the desert and the sown, to remain buying and selling or plying their trades for a month, or a season, or a year, or five years, either renting houses in the city proper or building reed wigwam settlements like gypsies in its suburbs. The average rent in Timbuctoo was the equivalent of 10 cents American per month for a large unfurnished room, 60 cents American per month for an entire house. For $2 a month one could rent a palace with stables, courts, and terraces.

I asked how many white European residents there were and of what nationalities. He counted them on his fingers, and here is the little table I made up with his help:

WHITE MALE POPULATION OF TIMBUCTOO

Military and administrative, including one school-
teacher and one doctor (French) 79
French storekeepers or traders 7
Syrian storekeepers or traders 2
Greek storekeepers or traders 1

Total, white males 89

WHITE FEMALE POPULATION OF TIMBUCTOO

Sergeant's wife 1
French storekeeper's wife 1
Doctor's wife 1
School-teacher's wife 1

Total, white females 4

I wondered if there was another city in the world today of nearly 100,000 population, however remote, which hadn't a single American, English, or German resident in it—no "Nordics." And not one single Christian prostitute or missionary.

The only American resident Commandant Fourré could recall having heard of, even before his time, was Leland Hall, who had lived a year there modestly in native style and had written a charming book of which he had a copy in the post library.

As we were looking over these figures I had jotted

down, he said, "*Mon dieu*, I had forgotten the postmistress! That explains itself, because she's always there." I said, "That's all right, sir. Statistical tables are always wrong."

He said, "Yes, but I've also left out our leading citizen, the famous Père Yakouba who was here before some of us were born and will still be here when most of us are gone away or dead. He's a great old man. You will be wanting to meet him first of all."

Indeed I was wanting to meet him, for it isn't often whether in Timbuctoo, Teheran, or Jersey City that one may meet a man who has become a mysterious world-wide legend—and this was the Père Yakouba who went into Africa a long generation ago as a young missionary monk of the Augustinian Pères Blancs (the White Fathers), quit his robes and the priesthood to go magnificently and completely "native," adopt the native ways of living, marry a black woman, beget progeny as fabulous and wide-flung as the children of Noah—and contrary to all so-called "moral probability" to become, instead of the ridiculous renegade outcast of fiction, the greatest official political adviser and authority on native languages in the entire history of Franco-African colonization. Now an old man, he still lived with the black wife of his youth in the old Negro city, but governors, generals, and high commissions came seeking his advice and wisdom from as far as Dakar on the coast and the interior borders of Lake Tchad.

A thousand mysterious tales had been told and written of his life, and I imagined him, as one so often does in the case of such legendary figures, a mysterious, eccentric patriarch who might have stepped out of the less respectable pages of the Old Testament—a man perhaps something like Moses, who also married an African Negress and had a dreadful quarrel with his family and snobbish sister Miriam. The Bible says that the Lord God of Hosts approved the union, but the chapter which recounts it is seldom read or preached from in Anglo-Saxon churches.

At any rate, I stood somewhat in holy awe of Père Yakouba. I asked Commandant Fourré how and at what hour it was best to approach him. He said that morning was the best time, that just now I would probably find him in Daviot's grocery store opposite the post office, and that if I didn't I could pick up a boy there who would take me to his house in the old city.

I thanked the commandant, took my leave, and wandered across the parade ground, peeping in at the post office for a look at the postmistress "who was always there," and there she was, a plump, motherly young woman at the stamp window. There was a big sign which said in French, Arabic, Tuareg, and various dialects:

PLEASE DON'T SPIT ON THE WALLS

TIMBUCTOO INTERLUDE

A French corporal and several white-robed black men were mailing letters, or asking for them, and not spitting on the walls, which were whitewashed.

The grocery store, with its shelves of cotton prints, novelties, canned goods, hardware, and tinware suspended from the ceiling, hoes, shovels, iron pots, resembled the general store of a ranch crossroads in Wyoming, except that in place of the stove, apple-barrel, and upturned cracker boxes, there was a central table with chairs, for gossip and refreshment. Robed Negro clerks lolled behind the counters, but no trade was going on, and the four whites who sat there talking and drinking bottled lemonade pushed me a glass and a chair, casually as cowboys do, without introductions, as if I had been dropping in every morning at that hour for the past ten years. There was a round-headed, hospitable little man who seemed to be Daviot the proprietor, a sergeant in shirtsleeves from the fort, a cropped-bearded young civilian who looked like Arthur Livingston or an English archeologist but turned out to be just an extraordinarily nice young Frenchman who subsequently took a fancy to Katie, and a robust red-cheeked old man in rawhide sandals, flowing Arab trousers, an old khaki coat, stocky and powerful, with twinkling blue eyes and a great white beard, a benevolent patriarchal bull disguised as Santa Claus—in short the legendary Père Yakouba in flesh and blood.

"So you are from New York," he said, interrupting my timid self-introduction. "Then you must know my friend G. Bong, that crazy one who came here on a camel."

"Bong? G. Bong?" I asked, embarrassed; New York was a large place and I had been away from it for quite a long time. . . . Again the Père Yakouba interrupted, "But yes, you must know him, G. Bong, the one-eyed strong one with curly hair who laughs and writes for all the journals."

So that was it. The Père Yakouba, for all his prodigious scholarship, pronounced American names as they do on the boulevards. Pair-shang—Veal-song—G. Bong —*alors*, Floyd Gibbons. Yes, I knew him. I had seen him last with Spike Hunt at Red Lewis's. Red had preached a sermon, and we had sung Methodist hymns.

"Ah," said Père Yakouba, "he didn't tell me that he was religious. He came knocking at my door one night at nine o'clock and though I was asleep I liked his face with the patch on it, and I said, 'How nice it is that you have dropped in just at our cocktail hour in Timbuctoo,' and I brought out all the bottles but set out only one glass, and said, 'Of course I mustn't ask you to join me in the drinking because you are an American and a dry.' And he said, 'Hell, I'm doubly dry because I have just come across the Sahara.' He had come, that crazy one, all the way

212

from Morocco on a camel, and not with any caravan, mind you, and he said he was going to Dahomey on a bicycle. Are you all crazy, you Americans, or just those of you who write and travel? By what strange means of locomotion, for instance, have you arrived?"

I confessed that I had arrived actually on a donkey, but only from the river landing, having come unadventurously up from the south on the Niger, so that it wasn't worth talking about.

"I suppose you will want to see my household too," he said. "Everybody does who comes here. When we were inundated with the first Citroën convoys, I painted a sign and put it up over my door:

"OUI, C'EST ICI. ENTRÉE 2 FRANCS. 50 CENTIMES DE SUPPLÉMENT POUR VOIR LA BÊTE EN LIBERTÉ SUR LA TERRASSE. (Yes, Père Yakouba lives here. Admission 10 cents. A nickel extra to see the animal at large on the roof.)

"But I had to take it down," he continued. "The commandant insisted that it wasn't dignified; so when you and Madame come the admission will be free. Of course you are a dry like G. Bong, even though you didn't arrive on a camel. So come both of you this afternoon at the hour for the *apéritif* a little before sundown. Pick up a boy to guide you, for otherwise you'll never find the house. But no, come to the store here with your wife at five o'clock—that will be simpler—and I'll meet you and we'll take a little walk first in the town."

So on the afternoon of our first day, it was the Père Yakouba himself who led us into the old mysterious city, padding through the streets of sand. Some were narrow and some were wide, but all were crazy-turning, in a labyrinth of clay-built houses and palaces, strong, rectangular like forts, all flat-roofed with terraces, their pilon-buttressed façades, usually without windows, sloping slightly backward like Egyptian tombs. The doors were tomblike, of heavy timber, sometimes brass-studded, sometimes burned or painted in arabesques. The rare small windows were of latticed wood. Open doorways of humbler houses were sometimes screened with mats or with curtains made of hide. Immediately on quitting the grocery store and parade ground, we had left behind everything modern or European. There are no glass windows in Timbuctoo, nor any electric lights or gas, nor any hotels or European houses, nor any street names or numbers, nor traffic cops, nor cinema, nor motor cars, nor advertising signs of any sort, even in Arabic.

Cars can come to Timbuctoo across the desert, but the only means of locomotion in its actual streets is on donkey-back, on horseback or camel-back, or afoot as we were going. There was little traffic of any sort in the streets through which we now were winding—occasional robed figures afoot or on donkeys, mostly black men and women, all barefooted, the women with enormous earrings of amber and gold, and occasionally we passed desert nomads of paler face.

We saw the principal mosque—there are three of them, all more or less alike—a rambling, shabby walled enclosure, also of clay and without domes, with a squat pyramidlike minaret, queerly decorated with wooden spikes stuck in the clay like a porcupine's quills, and surmounted by a gleaming ostrich egg.

Finally we emerged into the principal market place, the great bazaar on the northern edge of the city, and here for the first time found crowds and animation. There were long galleries with arched open booths in which the merchants and traders sat, and others who squatted with their wares spread out in the sand. The wares themselves were disappointing, merely foodstuffs and the commonplace objects of daily utility. There were no goldsmiths' or silversmiths' booths, no venders of fine rugs or curios such as lend color to the great bazaars of Stamboul and Damascus, no "turbaned merchants of the east" with rare incense, amber, jewels, or ivory. Père Yakouba explained that in Timbuctoo the merchants of precious things had neither booths in the bazaar nor shops anywhere, but trafficked privately, either by appointment in their own houses or more frequently bringing their wares to the home of the prospective buyer. This custom had continued traditionally from the days less than thirty years past when the Tuaregs used to raid the city so frequently that no man dared display real wealth in public.

But the market with its booths and crowds was now beginning to be flooded by a strange sunset glow that invested even the most common things with a queer, luminous, almost unearthly glory. Faces and robed men and women moving in it became glorified, apocalyptic, like dream figures in Jerusalem the Blest.

We had had a first experience of this unreal sunset glow, approaching Timbuctoo late on Christmas afternoon when we had come to a little river, deep, swift-flowing through the sand with thorn trees on its banks, which our pack donkeys had to swim.

There had been no one at the ford when we arrived there, but a leaky old canoe of hides stretched on wooden ribs lay opportune on the near bank for our crossing. This same unnatural glow filled the atmosphere, shimmering on the crystal waves and golden sand. There had been no soul at the river ford, but when we reached its farther bank a silent black man, naked to the waist and skirted, was standing there, who seemed unreal as the sunset, for a great two-handed battle sword, Crusaderhilted, hung at his side, and he was holding on a double leash two young gazelles, their necks encircled with wide, bright red leather collars. He was unreal as a dream in the unreal light, and I had an uncanny feeling that he and the two human-eyed gazelles were going to vanish in thin air when three tall women now appeared who seemed also of another world, for they were robed in flowing black like mourners in an ancient tragedy of kings; and their faces were the color of pale ivory; and all three were beautiful but only one was young and she was, so help me God, the most beautiful woman I had ever seen on earth except the dead Joan Martindale.

These things we had seen like a biblical vision, in sunset at the river ford, approaching Timbuctoo. Katie had seen them as I saw them, and as we rode on in the quick falling darkness, talking very quietly of what we had seen, we asked ourselves if it would not be better to turn our little caravan about and never enter the mysterious city.

It is not always wise to follow dreams. Twice in our lives we had set out for Samarkand, and each time we had failed, but kept our dreams. Baghdad, which we reached, had disappointed us both miserably, and we were wondering if Timbuctoo would be the same—if it could contain anything that would not efface this golden vision at the ford and leave shabby disappointment in its stead. But we had come some thousand miles by motor truck up from the Ivory Coast, across the High Volta and part of the Soudan, then some hundred miles by boat up the Niger, and finally this last few miles on donkeys from Khabara, and it seemed a little bit late to be turning back because we had seen a vision. . . .

And we had done well to continue on, for now with Père Yakouba, who had wisely chosen the same sunset hour to lead us into the old city, the same mysterious light had come again—and other women walked in groups with long black robes and faces of pale ivory, cameo cut; and there were other giants, half naked, black, with great Crusaders' swords, and again they seemed unearthly. Père Yakouba told us that these special women, notoriously beautiful as a race, and contrasting with the negroids as much in feature as pallor, were Peuhls, a people believed to be the scattered descendants of the ancient Egypt of the Pharaohs; that the black giants with the swords were Bellah slaves about the business of their Tuareg masters. There were Tuaregs also in the market, with their chins and mouths veiled, but their upper faces free, reddish-skinned like American Indians, with wicked noses and cruel eyes.

Contrasting with all these, and with the predominating naïve, coarser, kindly faces of the blacks, two beautiful young Arabs passed, young men, white-robed, with long

hair flowing on their shoulders. Their arms were en-
twined and they walked whispering alone in the crowd,
like Christ and the beloved disciple John at twilight by
the sea of Galilee. They walked in mystery and beauty,
with a troubled light in their soft eyes. Judas watched
them, jealous, with a little black goatish beard and a
leather bag at his waist. And Simon Peter passed with his
baskets and fishing-gear.

Close by our own side stood one older and more patriarchal than them all. Was it Ezekiel, that old prophet,
conjuring these visions for us? Or was it Père Yakouba
changing again into a legendary figure, although he had
invited us for cocktails?

We had forgotten all about the visit and the cocktails. I think he had forgotten too. I tried to tell him
of the tricks the changing magic light had been playing
on a susceptible new-come stranger. This queer glow in
the atmosphere of Timbuctoo, he said, with its amazing
range of luminosity and color, was due, he thought, to
the fact that the city, while set on the edge of the great
desert, was yet skirted on its western side by wide lagoons
and backwater creeks which washed southward into the
near immense swamps and lakes of the Niger. Later we
watched and studied the changing lights of dawn and
sunset, sometimes from Père Yakouba's roof in the old
city, sometimes from the terrace of our own caravanserai.

If one arises very early to go upon the roof under the stars, there comes a faint rose glow before the dawn. It fades, for it is the false dawn of which Omar Khayyám sang, and is succeeded by a deathly pale white grayness on the city walls, like the half light of the Elysian Fields which is followed by no dawn forever. One shivers, waiting, for the nights are cold in Timbuctoo, dogs bark, the pigeons and muezzins call, and the sun rises in its fiery heat. Toward sunset in the low slanting rays there is no heat or fire, but a long hour of soft, luminous golden glory, after which the walls of the city turn lavender and deepest glowing purple.

"It is a little late for cocktails now," said Père Yakouba as he led us back through the darkening maze of streets. "Boubekar will have your dinner waiting, and will come thinking you are lost. Everybody gets lost after dark in Timbuctoo. Come both of you tomorrow."

III

"I HAVE been meaning to mend this stairway for twenty years," said Père Yakouba, "but I have never dared to undertake it. If I once begin doing things like that, I'll mend the roof, put in glass windows, buy a bathtub, and a bed, and die in one of them, as I should well deserve, of rheumatism. The human mind is perhaps the only thing that doesn't risk being spoiled by improvement, and even that has its risks."

Père Yakouba's house, with this dark earthen stairway, was a robbers' cave and yet a palace, large and two-storied with its heavy walls of clay, with unlighted passages, ladders, mysterious inner courtyards where donkeys might be stabled and Ali Baba's jars of oil concealed. Transported to Central Park or Coney Island, children would go mad about it. Grown-ups dependent on steam heat, electric buttons, modern plumbing, might have wondered how even the donkeys could inhabit such a place in comfort, but happy people lived in it, which is not always true of palaces on Long Island and in Cincinnati.

221

In the lower court we had met Salama, the cherished wife of Père Yakouba's youth, now a big motherly black woman radiating competence and goodness, surrounded by female children and grandchildren, including a daughter suckling a new-born baby, other grown daughters sewing, while their naked brats played on the earthen floor. Still other married children with children of their own who might never see the patriarchal hearth in Timbuctoo were scattered like the tribes of Israel—a daughter married to a Scotch engineer in Australia, another teaching school in Madagascar, various sons in the service of the French-African government, another in the University of Paris, others engaged in commerce or professions in Europe. Salama herself, married to Père Yakouba in girlhood by both the Christian and the Moslem rites, had given him thirty sons and daughters. And here she sat, the great black mother, honored by her children, mistress of the household, robed like a fat old empress, with amber balls set in silver, big as walnuts, dangling from her ears, and golden anklets on her fat bare feet.

Life downstairs where Salama ruled went on in the purely classic way, untouched by Europe or by the frantic advertisements in the *Saturday Evening Post*—mats and rugs on the earthen floor, aged slaves pottering, cooking in the open courtyard where small beasts were stabled.

Upstairs on the second floor life was also classic, for

most of it was lived on the terrace roof, but it was classic in a double sense, for giving on the terrace was Père Yakouba's study and library with chairs, tables, pipe-racks, books, the lair of an old scholar into which he had led us up by an earthen staircase which hadn't been repaired for twenty years, but which contained volumes that would have been the despair of people who had acquired their automatic culture as well as their automatic ice-boxes by answering the frantic advertisements. I had known that Père Yakouba was a leading authority on Arab literature and African dialects—his specialty—but other shelves of old thumbed books attested a prodigious groundwork knowledge; Aristotle, Plato, and the Greeks were there, in Greek; the Latin poets and church fathers, in their Latin; the Old Testament in Hebrew and the New in Greek; German and Italian classics too, in German and Italian—and in English among great older names, *Huckleberry Finn*, *Gulliver's Travels*, *Uncle Tom's Cabin*, *Robinson Crusoe*.

On a small separate shelf were a dozen volumes, published in Paris, which he himself had written, the latest a technical work on the arts and industries of Timbuctoo which he had illustrated with his own sketches in pen and ink. I noticed that these books were all signed "Dupuis-Yakouba," and when he had taken us out on the terrace and had produced an array of bottles as formidable as his library and we sat drinking Berger and looking out over roofs of the city, I asked him about the double name.

"Dupuis," he said, "is my family name, and I'll tell you how I got the name of Yakouba—and how I didn't like it. The vicar general had taken out a number of us raw young monklings, still unaccustomed to our skirts, to introduce us to some Moslem dignitaries in the north. I was among the youngest and least of them. An old Cadi pointed to me and said, 'Who is that one?' We were speaking Arabic, and the vicar general, who scarcely knew me and who I am sure had never given a slightest thought to the name under which I should be ordained, replied, 'That is Père Yakouba.' You understand that Yakouba is Arabic for Jacob, and is a name never given in Arabic to any except a Jew.

"When we got back to the monastery college, I said, 'The Jews are God's chosen people and Jacob was a great man, but since I happen to be born a French Christian, I don't see why you want to make a Jewish monk out of me.' The vicar general laughed and said, 'The truth is I have no idea why that name popped out of my mouth, but I called you Père Yakouba, and Père Yakouba you will be.' So Père Yakouba I was, and Père Yakouba I have remained despite the fact that long ago I left the robes behind."

It occurred to me, though I didn't venture to say so, that perhaps the vicar general had chosen more prophetically than he knew, for Jacob, as all pious Bible students will recall, was a very great begetter. With the co-operation of not only his two wives, the sisters Leah and Rachel, but that of both their young handmaidens as well, he begat most of the tribes of Israel.

And Père Yakouba was no priest apostate who had quit the church on doubts or doctrines, but one who had left it honorably when he discovered that he was a man first and a monk afterward, and if he had become in turn as great a begetter as Jacob, he lived full of honors, and still communed with God.

It occurred to me also, with no stress on this one particular point, that Père Yakouba, the whole of him, as he sat there and I was beginning to know him, was that rarest of all white phenomena whether among the humble or the great—a happy man. His great kindness—he was kind, it seemed, to every one and was certainly being wonderfully kind to us—a kindness saved from being maudlin by a sense of humor that was sometimes whimsical and sometimes boisterous as a Rabelaisian bull, was perhaps one secret of his happiness. "Be good and you'll be happy." Lots of the silly copy-book platitudes prove true if carried to extremes deplored by Teacher.

At any rate, there he was. And he told us, among other

things, that he was never going anywhere else. Once in thirty years he had returned to Europe, Paris and his own native village near Château-Thierry, but had grown homesick for Timbuctoo and had cut short his visit. Persuaded to undertake a second one, he had gone a thousand miles down the Niger, thence to the port of Dakar, put his baggage on the steamer—and then fled back to Timbuctoo without even reclaiming the money for his ticket.

Only in Timbuctoo was he at home, but here he was completely so, and because he loved it, and was kind to us, we began to love it and even to understand it, if only ever so little, through him. On the afternoon following our visit to his house, he took me to call on his old friend the Cadi Achmed Baba Ben Sidi Labas, who, combining functions vaguely similar to those of mayor and judge, was the chief Negro personage of the city. He was a fat old man, very black and six feet tall, turbaned and swathed in robes of fine white linen, his breast covered with French medals. He spoke no French and had never seen Paris, but he was a Chevalier of the Legion of Honor and an Officer of the Academy as well. He and Père Yakouba—who never knew exactly what medals he had or hadn't received and never wore them—were like two old brothers. The Cadi insisted on my sitting on the huge, low, rug-covered divan, which was too much honor, seated

226

himself on a common three-legged stool, while Yakouba squatted on the divan's edge. Then, promptly and rightly, they forgot all about me. *Haec olim meminisse juvabit.* They were old men gossiping of the old great days, and I was nothing. They only became aware again of my presence when a servant brought in sweet drinks and honey-cakes. Then Père Yakouba told me something of his old friend's history which touched the final conquest by the French of Timbuctoo a generation earlier, and in which he also had played his rôle. Timbuctoo was then a free Moslem Negro city, but completely at the mercy of the Tuaregs, who raided and pillaged. These raids had become so frequent that the rich Timbuctooans disguised themselves and lived in the straw huts in the suburbs while the Tuaregs stabled their horses in the palaces. A dervish had told this Sidi Labis of a dream in which he had seen white men come up the river with purifying fire, after which the lion and the sheep lived peacefully in Timbuctoo together. Ben Sidi Labas went down the river and helped bring up the French. So they came, not conquering black Timbuctoo, but rather delivering it from the Tuaregs. Ben Sidi Labas, now the Cadi and God's servant, had helped both the French and his own black people, and had lived to reap rich rewards and honors. If Père Yakouba was Timbuctoo's leading white citizen, the Cadi was undoubtedly its leading black.

227

The Immam of the mosque whom we next visited—but who served only God and had no medals for it—took in sewing to eke out his livelihood. His house was humble and the mosque itself was shabby and run down, though worshipers still came, content as desert people are to say their prayers on any worn-out rug or mat. The richest house we visited, after the Cadi's palace, was that of the blacksmith, a skinny little Arab with a scraggly beard who in addition to being what we others call a blacksmith was a worker in all metals, including gold and silver. Katie had broken a pair of horn-rimmed or rather celluloid-rimmed reading glasses, and in the whole of French West Africa there is not a single optician. The blacksmith mended them in an hour by drilling microscopic holes through which he ran silver wire. There was no sign on the blacksmith's door and the lower part of his house was bare save for his tools in the interior court, but when we ascended to the upper story and the terrace we found him sumptuously installed. He brought out leather sacks and treasure chests from which he drew bracelets, rings, earrings, daggers, amulets, Tuareg padlocks, necklaces, and what not, mostly of his own fabrication, in silver, gold, and brass. We bought some of them at prices that were reasonable, but not cheap.

All native buying and selling except that of common objects in the bazaar and streets and such as went on in

228

the European general stores was thus carried on in private, as Père Yakouba had already explained to us. The whole of Timbuctoo, he said, was a "vast covered market," but no visitor would guess it by walking through the streets. With the trades and industries it was the same. No signs, no workshops, no industrial quarters, no ateliers were visible anywhere.

"People come," said Père Yakouba, "and go away saying we are a lazy lot who live in mud houses doing nothing all day long. They reproach us with it, but what a paradise if it were only true! Think of living without ever having to work. In Timbuctoo as elsewhere, we must work for our living, but we work in the interior courtyards of our own houses and never hang out shingles. We have carders and spinners and weavers of cotton and wool, dyers and embroiderers, tanners and cobblers and workers in fine leather, carpenters, masons, potters, basket-makers. During the hours when Timbuctoo seems deserted and the streets seem, as you said, like an Egyptian cemetery, all this is going on in the interior courtyards."

During succeeding days, he took us to see various of these individual craftsmen, all working by hand and with primitive or medieval tools. Sometimes we found them loafing, even napping shamelessly, always unhurried, seeming well contented with their work, taking a month if they chose to finish and polish and beautify an object that could be made—less beautifully—by machinery in a minute.

Thus Timbuctoo, which had seemed so mysterious and desolate on our arrival, became under Père Yakouba's guidance a living city of living people. As we sometimes rambled with him early mornings and late afternoons, he began interpreting the various street cries of the women peddlers and encouraging us to taste their wares. Everywhere from house to house women pass in the morning with baskets of *takula*, the bread of Timbuctoo which has been baked in domelike clay ovens, of leavened whole wheat, in the form of round disks about six inches in diameter and an inch or more thick. They cry in the dialect:

"Kara ha! Nda Yerkoy! Kara tyi alawa!" ("Yellow bread! Ho, by God! Yellow bread is the desire of all!")

The loaf costs two sous French, the equivalent of about half a cent American, and is delicious when warm from the oven, with melted butter or honey.

The women who sell *furme*, balls of bean flour browned in boiling grease like fried potatoes, cry:

"Furme! Ha! Nda salaman. Gomni go banda! Ya!" ("Bean balls! Ha! Peace and good health follow after.")

The peddlers of *alfinta*, little fried rice cakes, do not mention their wares by name. They cry simply:

230

"*Dyi-dyi dungo!*" ("They are hot and greasy!")

Likewise do the women who sell *me-korbo*, doughnuts dipped in honey, who cry:

"*Idye meyra yo!*" ("Hey, kids! Come and get it!")

There are also *alkatyi*, doughnuts in the form of the figure 8, cooked in butter and sugared, whose sellers cry, no matter what the season of the year:

"*Alkatyi! Ha! Me-ferkoy oy!*" ("Doughnuts! Eat 'em and break the vows of Ramadan.")

Merchants who sell bonbons of coarse flour and honey in which hashish is mixed cry honestly:

"*Har ber dobu, idye kayne ollondi.*" ("It is good for strong men, but folly for children.")

Toward sunset and through twilight with these and other peddlers crying and selling their small wares, Timbuctoo reaches its greatest animation, but almost immediately after night has fallen the entire city becomes a tomb. There are never any street lights, and usually by nine o'clock there is not a single light burning anywhere. It was this that had made us seem lost on the night of our arrival with the city actually under our noses. The same thing often happened, of course always as now in the dark of the moon, Père Yakouba told us, to people who had lived there for years. We were talking on his roof as the darkness fell. The young man who wasn't Arthur Livingston said it had happened to him once when he had gone hunting at night, with three Negro guards of the garrison who had been born in Timbuctoo and who thought they knew every stick and bush and hummock within a radius of miles. Night hunting around Timbuctoo, he explained, was engaged in with a tiny acetylene lamp, like a bicycle lamp, the reflector strapped to the forehead above the eyes, and the tube running to a tank in the pocket. The rays attracted beasts, and you saw just the glitter of their eyes without being able to distinguish the bodies. It was rather sporting, for you fired between the eyes, not knowing whether it was a rabbit or a lion, and sometimes, though rarely enough in recent years, it might turn out to be a lion. Usually it was a jackal. At any rate, the young man said, they had wandered five or six miles in the dark as they had often done before, but this time got lost on the way back, with their light used up, and couldn't find Timbuctoo. They were so completely lost that they lay down to wait for morning, and when dawn came they were on the edge of the commandant's vegetable garden—

"And not only that," interrupted Père Yakouba; "you can get lost here inside the town as easily. I will wager that without a lantern, and maybe even with one, you, for instance, can't find your way back from my house to the caravanserai after all the lights are out."

This seemed to me inconceivable. I had been back and

forth a number of times by now, though never in darkness without a lantern, and I thought I knew the streets, and even if I should miss a turning, it seemed that I ought to be able to guide my way out by the stars. We argued about it and finally wagered a bottle of champagne, and it was agreed that we would all four dine on Père Yakouba's roof the following evening, that the young man would see Katie back to the caravanserai with the lantern, and that I would try to get back on my own.

With the stars to help me, I was completely confident. In daylight, it took usually about a quarter of an hour, not more. They teased me and said, "Good-bye, we'll see you in the morning," and Père Yakouba offered me a blanket to keep me warm, sleeping in the sand. We waited the time for Katie to get back and put out the lights in the caravanserai as had been agreed. I started confidently, took a wrong turning somewhere, and was in narrow black passages between walls which all looked perfectly alike and which I had never seen before. I gave up looking for houses or familiar turnings, and wound my way by the stars, as nearly as I could in the general direction of the parade ground and the caravanserai. But I was in a labyrinth and had to go at zigzag angles. At last I got out of the maze into clear sand, and there was the desert, and there, low-lying, dark, across a couple of hummocks loomed what I took to be the caravanserai. But it seemed

233

farther away than it ought to be, and when I reached it, it was only another big sand hummock. I turned around and looked back, but where was Timbuctoo? Sand hummocks and black shadows everywhere, and all alike. The aggravating thing was that it was not perfectly pitch dark. I could see my hand before my face, and see things vaguely at a distance, for there was the desert starlight. But they looked all alike. I managed, by reversing my star route, to get back to the city's outskirts, but the outskirts I reached were not those I had left. I had started at nine o'clock for a fifteen minutes' walk. It was now past eleven, a match showed me on my watch dial, and I had learned my lesson. There was no sense in going back into the labyrinth, and still less sense in wandering off into the desert and losing even Timbuctoo. I sat down against a wall, and lighted a cigarette. The night was cold, but the dawn was beautiful. . . .

The champagne was too sweet for my taste, but Père Yakouba said it was excellent, and that if I wanted my *revanche* I could try it again and that he would wager a dozen bottles for encouragement—only he insisted that I take a pillow and a blanket.

IV

WE MIGHT have been in Timbuctoo for another month—or until now—despite the bats in the caravanserai, if Katie hadn't somewhat suddenly decided otherwise.

She decided, on what seemed to be the morning after New Year's Day, having plotted in the night with Yao, that we were seeing too much of city life and had better be starting back to the bush where I belonged.

She said, "William, I love Père Yakouba very much, and you know I like to see you enjoy yourself. You are both charming, up to certain limits, but the truth of the matter is that I think you are having a very bad influence on each other, and that we ought to go away. And if you want to know the whole truth, Salama thinks so too. She says she hasn't seen him in such a state since the last Fourteenth of July."

The day before had been New Year's Day, so far as I could remember, and we had planned to make a series of fashionable New Year calls—Katie, Father Yakouba, and I, and the young man who was neither Arthur Livingston nor an English archeologist—on the notables of Timbuctoo. The first call, around ten o'clock in the morning, was to have been on Colonel Fourré, the post commander who had shown us various attentions, including sending us lettuce and lending us some camels, and who would be receiving formally at that hour. I was to go and get Père Yakouba and we were to join Katie and the young man in the grocery store at nine-thirty. After calling on the colonel, we were to call on the High Cadi, on the Immam, on the blacksmith who had mended Katie's eyeglasses, the white lady doctor's wife, etc., etc. For the late afternoon we were invited to tea at the schoolteacher's with the promise of tennis.

Katie, with Boubekar's assistance, had pressed her nicest dress, and I had had a new pair of trousers made of which I was extremely proud, for they were just like Père Yakouba's, the loose Arab kind, very swanky, and had been made by Mamadou Machine, the leading tailor of the city, in exact replica of Père Yakouba's own. Mamadou, a fat black man, had his shop in a mud house that looked like a stable, but he had three sewing-machines—a Singer (pronounced San-jaire), a Vesta, and one of a German brand named Titan—and three grown sons who peddled them barefoot. One of the sons had accompanied me to Daviot's store where we bought and I paid for the cloth, buttons, findings, even the thread.

Then returning to the tailor shop we discussed the price for the work, with Père Yakouba controlling, so that it was agreed on at 9 francs (36 cents American). The trousers were ready for New Year and were a superb success.

So about nine o'clock on the morning of New Year's Day, having also put on a necktie for the second time in Africa, I wandered out into the sunshine to go and get Père Yakouba and bring him back to the rendezvous. The young man was to gather Katie. Passing the grocery store on my way, I thought it would be nice to take Père Yakouba a little New Year present and consulted Daviot, who said that a bottle of Amer Picon would be just the thing for New Year's.

Salama, as always radiating smiles and goodness, said Père Yakouba was on the roof awaiting me, and to go on up. This roof terrace was a delightful place in the morning, for it was protected by a high wall on the east for shade, and looked westward out over other roofs and terraces. But the school-teacher had also bethought him to send Père Yakouba a little New Year present, which chanced to be a bottle of Pernod and which stood unopened on the table with two glasses and a jug of water, awaiting my arrival. So that now there were two unopened bottles. They presented a problem. Père Yakouba pointed out that there would be a slight discourtesy to the absent school-teacher if we didn't open the Pernod, and a definite discourtesy to me if the Picon were left corked. So we decided to open them both and have a sip from each before going to join Katie and the young man at the grocery store.

Shortly afterward a little black boy came up on the roof with a note from Katie saying she was at the grocery store with the young man, and that it was already past ten o'clock, and that since we were going to the colonel's reception at ten o'clock, etc.

The little boy arrived inopportunely, for Père Yakouba had brought out the Latin text of Saint Augustine's *Confessions* and was expounding the curious chapter in which the saint tells of how he had only been saved from becoming a Pantheist in Rome by worrying over how a sparrow could contain as much God as an elephant. So we sent Katie profound apologies for our tardiness, and said for her and the young man to go ahead to the colonel's reception, and that we would join them there.

We had invented meanwhile, incidentally, a refreshing beverage which, so far as I am aware, though fairly obvious, has never been experimented with in other non-prohibition centers. It consisted of Amer Picon and Pernod in equal parts, with a dash of water added. It is pleasing because the Picon is bitter, while the Pernod alone is much sweeter than old-time absinthe was, and hence slightly cloying.

A short time later another little black boy appeared, accompanied by Yao, who was dressed for New Year's in a suit of white ducks I had given him and who also was wearing a necktie. He said that Madame had got tired waiting and had gone with the young man to the colonel's reception, and that she was *fachée même beaucoup*, and that what I was doing was *pas bon*.

Yao's arrival was likewise inopportune, for we had progressed from Saint Augustine to other mystic Church Fathers, including Saint Thomas Aquinas and had been discussing his learned speculations concerning the anatomy of the more intimate physical parts of angels, involving the problem of whether angels are able to couple with each other, as the devils do, or only with the daughters of men. So we told Yao to go to the colonel's reception himself, at least as far as the door, and find Madame Katie and explain to her nicely that it would be impolite for us to come to the colonel's reception so late, but that we would meet her and the young man at the grocery store afterward and all go together to call on the Cadi, the Immam, and the blacksmith who had mended her eyeglasses.

A very short time later another little black boy came, and this time brought the young man who wasn't an Eng-

239

lish archeologist but who spoke rather good English in
spite of it, and who said that it was now noon of New
Year's Day, too late to call on anybody else, and that
Katie had gone back to the caravanserai for lunch and
had said for me and Père Yakouba to go to hell.

We had eaten a snack of goat cheese and some bread-
flaps on the roof, but the mention of lunch made us
hungry again, and the sun was straight up in the air; so
we decided to go into the library, and Salama sent us up
a bowl of stew from downstairs, and we ate some of it,
and decided that it would be nice to take a little nap before going to get Katie and the young man to pay the
rest of the calls in the afternoon. So we lay down on
some nice mats on the library floor to take a nap.

After a while another little black boy came, and woke
us up, and he had brought Katie, and the young man,
and Yao—and also Salama. Salama and Katie had evidently been talking about us behind our backs, which is
not a nice thing for wives to do, and always leads to un-
pleasantness. Salama said some things to Père Yakouba
which I couldn't understand, but I think they were somewhat the same things Katie was saying to me, that it was
now half-past five and that New Year's Day was over,
and that we had promised to call on a lot of people, and
there we lay on the floor. We were not lying on the floor
like that, we were lying on nice mats, having taken a nice

nap. We weren't just lying there the way it sounded when Katie and Salama said we were lying there. But they were unreasonable, and made more of it than it really was.

Fortunately some other people came to call on Père Yakouba, and we all went out on the terrace, which was now cool and lovely again. Père Yakouba was sweet to every one and asked Katie and Salama please not to scold us, and we all had some vermouth and it was beautiful on the roof, and there were people singing Arab songs and playing the lute on other roofs, and presently the muezzins began calling from the minarets, and Katie smiled and drank some more vermouth herself and was as sweet as I have ever known her in my life. And when it got dark and Yao lighted the lanterns and we went back to the caravanserai, she was still just as sweet to me as she had been with the other people present, and didn't say anything more to me about the calls at all.

It was only next morning, after letting me sleep as late as I liked, and after our breakfast coffee and cigarettes, that I noticed Yao was beginning to pack up things.

Another donkey caravan, more water travel on the Niger, our motor-truck rejoined at Mopti, and before the week was ended we were chugging southeastward to-

241

ward the mountains, past the Palisades of Bandiagara, toward the heights where dwelt—or so we had been told —the legendary Habbe, cliff-dwellers and phallic worshipers, least-known and strangest race in western central Africa.

PART FOUR

MOUNTAIN PEOPLE

I

I<small>T WAS</small> the encyclopedic Dr. Johnson who once wrote
a book describing a country in which the wives rode
out to war while the husbands stayed at home in
bed giving birth to and suckling the babies. Since this,
however, was contrary to respectable British precedent—
and since furthermore the country could never be located—it was reasonably concluded that he was pulling
the legs of the English.

I hasten, therefore, to set down that the mountains and
cliffs of the Habbe—a people certain of whose customs
may seem as topsy-turvy as those described in *Rasselas*—
can be easily located on any big map of Africa by draw-
ing a pencil line straight east from Bandiagara and another pencil line straight south from Timbuctoo; the
Habbe inhabit the territory at the point where your pencil lines cross. Furthermore, if you decide to go there, you
can go almost the whole way up from the West Coast
by motor truck, thanks to the heroic road-building
mania which the French colonials have inherited from

Julius Caesar, who built roads to just as incredible places
when Gaul was as savage as Africa.

But arriving there, you will be, for once, at the end of
the road and at the end of the world, the "jumping-off
place," so far as modern vehicles are concerned, for the
landscape suddenly drops off into space and becomes perpendicular. You can drop a pebble that will fall a mile.
And it will drop past thickly inhabited towns, clinging
like nests of barn swallows.

It is a mad landscape with these towns built on the
perpendicular, with its cliffs, palisades and gorges, sub-
terranean tunnels, honeycombed caves, ropes, endless
steep stone staircases as miraculous as Jacob's Ladder to
the sky.

But it is not merely this landscape that will make you
doubt your wits and suspect that you have been transported by a violent fourth-dimensional Einstein trick to
another planet. It is that the people who inhabit this
topsy-turvy land are also topsy-turvy mad in certain fundamental attitudes toward life—that is, *if we are sane.*

You will discover this only gradually, but from the
very first you will begin to see things, as we did, that will
set you wondering.

Climbing up through rocks and badlands by a serpen-
tine road approaching Sangha, a city which though built
by primitive African Negroes looked weirdly like an old

crusaders' stronghold with its walls and turrets, we passed a great stone altar from which rose a somewhat startling clay-sculptured object ten feet tall which not even the most learned professor or the most innocent elderly spinster could by any chance have mistaken for a Maypole, obelisk, or Cleopatra's needle. And installed an hour later on the terrace of the house that had been prepared for us, we faced another pedestal there in the sunshine, public as a statue of Gustavus Adolphus, and this one, considerably taller than a man, was even more surprising, for it was sculptured physiologically complete with its two natural spherical appurtenances large as bushel baskets. Its proud point was decorated tastefully with grass and wild flowers; and young Endyali Doli, who had escorted us to the house and sat with us on the terrace, explained that it was the "children's altar" and that children of the town had carried the flowers there in celebration of a recent religious ceremony. He himself had taken flowers there, he said, when he was circumcised.

Endyali was the twenty-one-year-old son of old Dounairon Doli, master of Sangha and chief of the Sangha clan, to whom we had brought letters and recommendations and who had been expecting us. The arrival of our motor truck on the edge of Sangha had caused a friendly commotion, and a shouting crowd had escorted us directly to Dounairon's house, which was a two-story castle built of stone and clay, with high-walled courtyards and stables within the court. The old man, who had been sick and was still temporarily bedridden on a fine fur-covered couch, was glad to see us, for in addition to the letters, we had brought medicine, a hundredweight of salt, a bolt of cloth, and a large porcelain soup tureen which we had learned at Bandiagara he had been wanting for a year or more, having broken one which a traveling German ethnologist had given him in 1911. The letters as well as the soup tureen came from Monsieur Maugin, French administrator at Bandiagara, who had long been friends with the Doli family, though they hadn't seen each other for years.

It was really for Maugin's sake that we were welcome. And Dounairon's notions of hospitality were as large and medieval as his castle. These were true African Negroes, so-called primitives, more isolated from civilization and white colonial influence than even the forest blacks of the thickest jungle, but they were not like any blacks or primitives I had ever known or read about. The interior of Dounairon's house—the mode of living they had independently evolved, as well as their castlelike exterior architecture—suggested the rude, copious feudal life of Europe in early medieval times. Dounairon had fine horses stabled in his court; bright-colored brass-studded saddles and bridles hung from wooden pegs in the eaves;

heavy wooden tables and heavy stools; beds covered with the skins of furry beasts; serfs, granaries, elaborately irrigated gardens and fields in green places among the rocks. The notables here wore robes, and the peasants belted smocks. I repeat that they were like primitive Negroes displaced in time and space to a mountain stronghold district in early Europe.

Dounairon was saying, "A house has been prepared for you in Sangha and a cook has already been installed. I am sick, as you can see, and cannot do personally for you all that I would wish, but I give you my horses and my son to be completely at your disposal so long as you remain in the Habbe country. Whatever you need, you will tell him, and all that you wish to see, he will show you."

Endyali was a smiling, black, plump-cheeked young man with the tiniest wisp of a little beard in the middle of his chin, a tight-fitting embroidered cap, white robe, and shoes of colored leather. He was very intelligent, exquisitely polite, particularly to Katie, and spoke not only perfect Bambara but an excellent pidjin. It was he who led us to our house and superintended our installation. He had a nice manner, and Yao, the "colonel," my badly spoiled Ivory Coast chauffeur who usually sulked when he had to take orders from a man black like himself, hustled about, whistling and approving, helping fix the beds, filling the carbide lanterns, joking with Katie, making friends with the cook, and telling me that we had *"ben tumbé,"* that it was *"bon—beaucoup même."*

The house was one that had been built in anticipation that Sangha might one day have a white resident from the Haute Volta administration. As a matter of fact there were no whites in Sangha or anywhere in the cliffs east of Bandiagara, nor had there been any except rare visitors for years. We were on the northern edge of the town, our house surmounting a small rocky promontory with a splendid view from the terrace out over the sloping, rocky badlands up which our truck had climbed. Endyali explained that while we had come up this long gradual slope to Sangha, the other side of the city overhung the sheer cliffs. To go down to the foot of the cliffs on horseback, he said, required an all-day journey, a detour of twenty miles. But by the tunnel and staircase, or by the ropes and notched ladders, one could descend on foot in a couple of hours. We hadn't seen anything yet of the real Habbe country, he kept assuring us. He would begin showing us tomorrow. He advised that we make the first trip on foot by the staircase. Later we could make as many longer journeys as we liked on horseback.

The cliff edge to which Endyali led us next morning disclosed a landscape which seemed like a distorted yet beautiful stage-set erected by giants who had dreamed

250

about *The Cabinet of Doctor Caligari*, the paintings of Picasso, the ramparts of Carcassonne, and had jumbled them all together in some secret place of their own hidden among the mountains on the other side of the moon. I am no good at describing landscapes, and nowhere else on earth is there anything like this Habbe landscape, or anything to which it can be sensibly compared. It seemed an incredible accident that these blacks in the interior of Africa had evolved by pure utilitarian chance this fantastic style of architecture with its fictitious resemblance to the romantic feudal style as depicted in books of fairy tales—ramparts, towers, bastions, and fortress walls, but clinging to ledges on the sheer cliffs, like nests built by wasps or birds, and looking like Howard Pyle drawings tilted out of perspective, like Maxfield Parrish castles in the clouds, like bad romantic wood-cuts made by incompetent and drunken English engravers a generation ago for *Idylls of the King*. The buttressed towers in which might dwell Merlin or Guinevere or the Lady of Shalott were really granaries, the culverins which projected from the embattled walls were merely wooden drains, the blunt-pointed towers were thatched with straw, the resemblance was all pure hazard, but it was astounding. And this whole topsy-turvy tilted landscape was thickly populated. At one point, descending the staircase, we came out from a narrow defile, tunnel-like, to an open ledge, halfway down the Sangha cliff, which gave a view of the curving face of the palisades for miles, and Endyali pointed out towns clinging there, some near, some distant, telling us the names of the largest, which we would later visit: Ireli, Ibi, Aru.

I kept repeating dumbly to him and to Katie, "But by God, there's nothing like this on earth anywhere." And Yao, the colonel, who had trailed with us (he had been totally unimpressed and scornful in Timbuctoo), kept muttering now to himself in his own Baouli tongue, like a man who was scared, and saying to Katie or me from time to time, "*Bon dieu! Bon dieu! Bon dieu!*"

I might as well leave it at that, leave the word to Yao, for that was the way it was.

Who were they, these strange Negroes, these Habbe, living among all these strange anachronisms, visible and invisible—still clinging to old Fetiches, I had been told, yet building altars of a formalized and fully developed phallic cult like that of the ancient Egyptian and Syrian Priapic sects—living in honeycombed cliff caves like Pueblo Indians, yet building robber-baron castles that were like a distorted dream of chivalry?

The Habbe have no written history, but they have a fixed tradition similar to that of the Old Testament Hebrew Exodus in the sense that it recounts a probable

252

actual historical hegira, embellished with purely legendary miracles and marvels. We had arrived among them
late in January, having been informed of the com-
memorative date beforehand, at the season approaching
the annual dances which pantomime the ancient history
of their forest origin and their wanderings from the low-
lands to these mountains. This story, which they outlined to us in order that we might understand the meaning of the dances, was that the Habbe were originally a
forest people, defeated and driven out of their country in
the ancient wars by the invading black conqueror Samori.
With their women and children, bag and baggage, and
with their ancestral Fetiches, they had wandered until
they came to the banks of the wide-flowing Niger, where
a band of crocodiles came out of the water miraculously
and transported them to the other side on their backs.
Resuming their wanderings, guided and forced to go on
by their Fetiches and witch-doctors, saved from their pur-
suers, but soon in a barren land where they underwent
terrible hardships of hunger and thirst, they arrived at
last at the foot of these cliffs and mountains. The tribe
camped on the slope, while Nangaban, the great tribal
hunter, accompanied by his two dogs, went up ahead. He
and his dogs wandered among the rocks, were lost for days
and on the point of dying from thirst, when they reached
a great pool from which a spring gushed, the pool swarm-

ing with crocodiles. Despite the fact that the crocodiles
of the Niger had saved the Habbe, Nangaban was on the
point of doing battle with these in order that he and his
dogs might drink and afterward have meat for the tribe.
But the dogs rushed into the water and began lapping it,
and Nangaban withheld his spear when he saw that the
crocodiles did not harm the dogs, but let them drink
peacefully. He also drank and presently bustards and
baboons came to drink. These he killed, returned to
the tribe, recounting the miracle, and led them up
into the mountain, for the Habbe had reached the end
of their wanderings and had come to their promised
land.

Establishing themselves there and beginning to explore
the neighboring cliffs, they had found them inhabited by
friendly cave-dwellers, a people of superhuman origin
whose ancestors had had wings, and whose religion was
this phallic cult with its great Priapic altars. The Habbe
settled and intermarried among them, adopted the new
religion without entirely relinquishing their old Fetiches,
built houses on the cliff tops and ledges, made common
community and common cause with the cave-dwellers
against invading Peuhls (a nomad race of legendary
Egyptian origin who may possibly form the connecting
link with the Eastern Priapic cults), and finally became
one people.

The dances which we saw at Sangha represented with costumes and pantomime these legendary, and possibly historical, events. They were totally different from anything I had ever seen among Fetichist or Voodoo blacks, and the masks were likewise radically different from anything I had ever seen in the forest. They were not carved "false faces," as the Congo and Ivory Coast masks are, but highly stylized tall headpieces, sometimes only incidentally covering the face, painted in brilliant colors. The forms were symbolic rather than ever literal. Some of them might have been designed by the Cubists and Surréalistes for an ultra-modern ballet. The dancers, for instance, who represented crocodiles wore wooden helmets surmounted by tall swastika-like double crosses, several feet tall, and nearly as wide, which at first glance suggested mechanical signals on railroad towers, and which one only realized gradually might represent the essence of "crocodile" in the same abstract way that certain Brancusi woods and marbles may represent the essence of "bird." Other masks represented, but always more or less abstractly and symbolically, ancestors, enemies, antelopes, hyenas, bustards, rabbits, peoples and animals of various sorts. As weird as any, in a different way, were the masks that represented the enemy Peuhls. They were hoods of brown, close-woven netting which covered the entire head and neck, like the hoods of the

Penitentes and the old Florentine religious companies, with the eyeholes outlined in white cowrie shells.

The dancing itself, which took place in broad daylight with firing of muskets and great crowds in the big public square of Sangha, was not frenzied or orgiastic, but as abstract and highly stylized as the costumes. These dances were not being done to please or instruct us. The Habbe were about their own business. We would have understood nothing of what the formalized gyrations and processions symbolized had it not been for the previous explanations, which made us understand a little. We were welcome and were being treated with the most generous kindness, but we found a great deal of it bewildering. We were strangers, and in a very strange land.

II

"**B**UT look here," said Endyali patiently, but eyeing me as if he thought I was very dull of comprehension, "nobody wants to marry a girl until she has shown that she can have a baby. Everybody knows that. She might be no good, and how can anybody tell until she has tried? If a girl refuses to lie naturally with the youths when she reaches the proper age for it, or fails to get big, having lain with them, it is a public shame on her and a shame on her family. Her mother can scold her all she likes, but a girl of that sort will never make a good wife or be good for anything. Besides, if you haven't lain with the girl yourself, how can you tell she is the one you want to marry? Besides, your father and mother wouldn't let you marry a girl who might be barren. They have the family to think about.—Isn't it the same where you came from?"

I gasped a little and told him that where I came from it wasn't quite the same. We were sitting in the Boys' Club of Sangha—both guests there through an invitation we had procured from a kid named Dano, one of Endyali's fourteen-year-old cousins. Dano and a number of other boys ranging in age from fourteen to fifteen or so had opened the clubhouse for us and had been showing us around. Endyali, who had been a member of the club but had been dropped from membership automatically when he reached full manhood, had been explaining to me its nature and functions. I had been having some difficulty in following him, particularly with reference to the status of young lady visitors, and was wondering whether I hadn't misunderstood him. He had begun by telling me from his own personal experience how the Habbe boys were initiated into the social group of "small grown-ups" and inducted into the club from which they were later dropped as he had been when they became "big grown-ups" and married. It had happened when Endyali was about fourteen. The Habbe, though Negro, are a tough, sturdy highland people, and it was around that age that he with a dozen or more other Sangha boys had attained full puberty and gone through the initiation.

"It is always the same way," he said. "It begins with circumcision, called *sendi-you*. We are first washed, purified, and instructed by the Hogoun, the high priest, given each a clean new smock, and then sent, the whole crowd of us, to a new straw house which has been built out on the rocks there, away from the town. In Sangha the drums beat all night for us, and we feel proud and important.

Next morning the *kekenendou*, the blacksmith, comes and circumcises us all with an iron razor. Women and girls can't come near the straw house or even look at it. When they go past they must turn their faces away. But our fathers or older brothers come and bring us all sorts of good things to eat, chicken, honey-cakes, milk, millet mush. There is a fence built round the straw house so that we can go out and sit on the rocks, but we can't leave the inclosure in the daytime until after we are completely cured. When it gets dark the drums come, beating so that all the women will go indoors, and take us back into town each night in procession, marching past the houses, where each boy is dropped at his own house, and sleeps there. But before dawn the drums come again and take us back to the straw house.

"When we are cured we run wild and free, rejoicing, for three days and nights, shouting, doing anything we like, and no one has the right to interfere with us or scold us. Everybody shuts up his chickens then, for we make wooden spears and have the right to chase and kill any chickens we can find. At night we build a bonfire out on the rocks and roast them. And we can come back and shout through the town and keep everybody awake, and people must give us presents. For those three days and nights we can do everything that we used to get scolded and beaten for when we were smaller."

Endyali laughed out loud as he told me about it, and I thought what a grand gang of little hoodlums they must have been during those three days of freedom, and of what would happen to grocers' carts and delicatessen stores if we adopted Habbe customs in New York.

"At the end of three days," Endyali continued, "we must stop running wild and walk about gravely with dignity, saluting our elders decently, to show that we have become 'small grown-ups.' The drums beat again, and we must go in company to make the sacrifices which complete our initiation. We are not permitted to have any help in this from the 'big grown-ups.' We must pound millet in a mortar, mix the flour with warm water, make a cream of it, put it in calabashes and carry it in procession to the children's altar which you saw out yonder, and pour it on the *toro* [the ten-foot erect phallus sculptured in clay]. After that we must make another sacrifice which is not so easy and with bad luck may take several days to finish. Each of us must go out with a weapon which we have made ourselves, so that it is usually a wooden spear or a little bow and arrow, and each of us must kill some wild thing and bring it back and pour its blood upon the *toro*. It makes no difference whether it is a baboon or a big animal, or just a little ground squirrel or a pigeon. But it must be some wild thing which we have killed ourselves.

"When this is finished we go hunting wild flowers, make a wreath of them for the *toro*—and after that we are admitted here at the club into the rank of the 'small grown-ups' and can sleep here when we like and can invite the girls we like best to come and sleep with us. We have first to ask their mothers. We still live at home and work for our parents and are nourished by them, but we can live in the clubhouse too whenever we choose, and often make our own feasts here. The girls who are invited cook for us, and wash the dishes, and afterward we tell stories and sing songs, and we pretend that we are really grown up now instead of just 'little grown-ups.' In the morning the girls must go home to their mothers."

The club quarters through which Endyali and his cousin and the other boys had been showing me consisted of a big house with walled courtyard and contained a big dining-room with little tables and stools, a sort of community kitchen with a hearth and cooking-utensils, numbers of individual rooms, including little bedrooms, like the cells of a monastery with wooden couches covered with skins and blankets. But though equipped as well as any house for real grown-ups, it remained a playhouse for kids, and they were free there. They had scratched their drawings all over the walls; they had their own secrets; there was a room they wouldn't let Endyali enter since he was now grown up; there were musical instruments scattered about, made by themselves, not unlike the cigar-box "guitars" we used to make when I was a kid; there were little chests which they wouldn't let us look into, but which I felt sure must contain jackknives, marbles, kites, and tops, or whatever their Habbe equivalent might be. It was, in fact, a good deal like the "club" which a gang we called Bob Conrad's Army had installed in an abandoned ice-house which belonged to Bob's father in Winchester, Virginia. We wouldn't let any grown-ups enter it. We had secrets, passwords, signs and conclaves, and an old stove on which we used to roast potatoes and sausages. We used even sometimes to invite our pigtailed sweethearts for these feasts, and they were properly awed and grateful and crossed their hearts never to tell. But if one of them had stayed out all night, or gone home with her dress or pigtails seriously mussed—well, there'd have been lanterns and bloodhounds and steam whistles, and fire and brimstone from Heaven.

Here, on the contrary, as Endyali was patiently explaining to me, young sweethearts were encouraged to lie together, and when the natural consequence followed for the girl it was a cause for family pride and congratulation. When the baby itself arrived, it was welcomed with even more pride and rejoicing.

If the girl had been popular, Endyali said, and a virtuous girl by Habbe standards, she had probably lain with various youths, so that the baby was considered to be all her own and to belong to her and to her family. She would nurse it and care for it in her parents' house, and it would have her family name. When she married later, she could take it with her to her new home or leave it in her parents' household, as she chose. But in either event it remained in name and fact a member and part of the parental household group, and when grown up in its turn, it would inherit from its mother's family.

Having shown that she can have a healthy baby, the girl is now eligible for marriage, and is usually asked in marriage by the favorite youth among those with whom she has lain, so that in choosing each other they know what they are about. They marry because they have found that they are suited to each other and like each other best. But once married, Endyali said, they must be faithful to one another—so long as they remain married. I asked him what he meant by remaining married, whether there was divorce among the Habbe? He said that either husband or wife had the right to divorce at any time, either for a reason or a whim, but that having experimented and chosen the mates they preferred, divorce was very rare. He had been explaining patiently and as best he could things which he found difficult to explain because they seemed to him so obvious, natural, and right as to require no explanation. It was impossible to discuss comparative social-sexual systems with Endyali because he didn't know about other systems, and he was such a nice young man that I felt it would not be right to shock him by telling him of ours.

I learned also somewhat later, quite by accident, that certain other Habbe social laws, those relating for instance to theft and murder, were mad and topsy-turvy too—that is, if we are sane.

In looking for a shiny dangling box of Katie's that contained face-powder, mirror, make-up, and that had been misplaced or had disappeared, we discovered that a number of other objects, curiously assorted, had also disappeared, in fact almost surely been stolen. One never locks up things. They just lie about. Doors and windows are always open, day and night. One never thinks about it. And we discovered that some things had disappeared —two red-labeled cans of tomatoes, a belt, a bottle of Worcestershire sauce, the coat to a bright-colored pair of pajamas. We hesitated to say anything about it—the value of the things was trivial—but we were going to be there for a number of weeks, and it gave us an uncomfortable feeling. So I decided to mention it to Endyali. He was vexed and said, "Ah, it's disgusting. The little children, the little ones, they are worse than monkeys.

You must tell your cook to drive them away and keep them away."

I said, "But how can you be so sure it was children?"

He looked at me, puzzled, and said, "But grown-up people don't steal."

I found this a bit difficult to swallow even in his topsy-turvy land. I said, "Hey, Endyali, there are thieves everywhere in the world. You don't mean to tell me that all the Habbe are honest? It couldn't be possible. What do you mean?"

He said, "Oh, there are bad people, of course, bad Habbe, some bad people everywhere. But they wouldn't risk doing a thing like stealing those objects from your house. It's too dangerous, not worth it; the punishment for theft is death."

"Not for stealing a can of tomatoes?"

"But yes, for stealing anything. It has to be that way. All our wealth is open. Even our granaries have only wooden locks; we leave our tools in the fields, our saddles and bridles on the limbs of trees. If people stole from each other, life would be impossible. Besides, a man who steals once will steal always. A thief is better out of the way. So when a thief is caught he is taken before the Hogoun and hanged the next morning. It's a very good law. It is only once in a long time that anybody is foolish enough to break it. No man in his senses would risk his life, for instance, to steal your belt or a can of tomatoes. That's why I am sure it was the little children."

"So really," I repeated, "the Habbe law punishes a man with death for stealing even a can of tomatoes, or a shirt, or a bridle or a tool left in the fields?"

"Yes," he repeated again, "for stealing anything."

"Well, if you hang a man for petty thievery, how in the name of God do you punish a murderer?" I demanded. "Do you boil him in oil or burn him alive or cut him up into little pieces?"

"Oh, that is altogether different," Endyali said. "A thief is no good, never any good. But any man, the most honest, may have the misfortune to be carried away by anger and kill another. My father might. Or you and I might get into a quarrel and one of us kill the other; yet we are honest men. So when a man has the misfortune to do murder, he is not exactly punished at all. He has to do penance, and is purified. How? Well, some of the older ones who have seen it can tell you about it better than I can."

Old Dounairon, still in bed, glad to be diverted by our visit, pleased to see that Endyali and I had become inseparable and were getting along so well together, said: "I will tell you, then, what happened in the case of the gardener Yaro, for that was a case I knew all about. He killed a man named Kogu Endou who was a cousin of our family, so that I remember it well. One evening, after the summer rains had ended and during the period when we were all busied with the cisterns and ponds in the rocks from which we irrigate in the later dry season, people came running here to the house to tell me that Yaro had just come in from the fields, waving his arms, crying and shouting that he had murdered his neighbor Kogu Endou—it had been a quarrel about an irrigation channel—and that he was on his way to the Hogoun. To understand our customs in such matters, you must know that they came to me not as mayor or chief of Sangha, but simply because Kogu was a man of our family and I was the family's head. My powers concern the material affairs of the clan, but the Hogoun as high priest is master of all matters which concern life and death, the spirit and the soul; so naturally it was to him that Yaro must go.

"My duty in the matter was only a family one, to go first and condole with the family of Kogu, who had been killed, and then to condole with the family of Yaro, who had killed him. The women of the two families, including Kogu's mother and Yaro's mother, joined together and bemoaned the whole night long, consoling each other, bemoaning Kogu and bemoaning Yaro.

"The next day Yaro, the murderer, who had been praying all night with the Hogoun, appeared before the assemblage of both families, and we cried with him and condoled with him, and mourned for him and for Kogu, saying, 'Alas, an ill thing has befallen Yaro and an ill thing has befallen Kogu.'

"The mother of Yaro and the mother of Kogu then prepared food for Yaro, and we all embraced him and wept with him, for his misfortune was very great, and bade him a long farewell, for Yaro must go on a long journey, leaving our mountains, and must remain wandering in exile for three years, and whenever people might say to him, 'Who art thou?' he must weep and reply, 'Alas! I am that Yaro who murdered Kogu in the fields at Sangha, and I am also as one dead.'

"For during the three years that Yaro was wandering in exile, we all said in Sangha that Yaro was dead. But at the end of the three years, and on the day when he had committed the murder, our families again re-assembled, for on that day we knew that unless some other fate had overtaken him, Yaro would return from the dead to be purified. On the afternoon of that day, toward the evening, the Hogoun sent drummers through Sangha, announcing that the needful had been done, and that Yaro was returning from the dead.

"This is how he returned, as all men must who have done a murder. He returned wearing a shroud, a burial garment of fine white cloth with blue stripes, holding with one hand to the tail of a black bull, which was led through the crowd by servants of the Hogoun, and holding in his other hand a piece of salt, while the crowd cried, 'Behold, it is Yaro returning from the dead. When Kogu returns also, everything will be as it was before.'

"Arriving where our two families were assembled, Yaro was welcomed and embraced and presented the piece of salt and the shroud to Kogu's mother. The bull was sacrificed and the two families feasted together, saying, 'Kogu also must return and then everything will be as it was before.'

"For Yaro, it was now all finished. He was purified, his brothers gave back to him the house and the fields which they had tended for him in his absence, and people embraced him and said, 'Ah, what you have suffered!' For it is a terrible misfortune to have killed one's neighbor, and now the misfortune had been lifted from him by purification.

"For Kogu, however, there was much yet that had to be done. Kogu must be restored to life by blood of Yaro's family, since it was Yaro who took the life, but in Kogu there must also be blood of his own family; else he would not be Kogu. In the family of Kogu, the Hogoun chose Kogu's brother, Bomo Endou, and since Yaro had no unmarried sister, the Hogoun selected the young girl of his nearest blood, a niece named Sada. These two lay

269

together until a child was conceived, and into this child, as it was being born, the Hogoun invoked the soul of Kogu, so that the soul of Kogu might enter into its new body and thus be restored to us again and life in Sangha. It was named Kogu, and in growing up would inherit all that was Kogu's. Thus the murder is wiped out, there is forgiveness, and everything is as it was before."

I thanked Dounairon and thought that of all the methods devised by humanity, civilized or uncivilized, to deal with homicide, this one was the strangest. I thought of the customs of certain other mountain people who made their own laws, for instance the mountain people of Corsica, of Sicily, of Kentucky, of the Carolinas, where whole feudist families are wiped out to avenge one original killing, and murder breeds murder for generations. I thought also of our statute laws, our lethal chambers, gallows, guillotines, electric chairs. I began wondering what fantastic things might happen if we changed our statutes and tried to apply the Habbe law in New York or Chicago. A worse orgy of murders, doubtless, than we now have? Probably yes, because we have developed a professional criminal class, professional killers. But I wonder exactly what a tough gorilla or a hired gangster who contemplated putting somebody on the spot would do if the law said to him, "Look here, we won't hang you or burn you, or even lock you up, but if you kill that fellow you've got to go and find his mother and tell her how sorry you are, and she will cry and tell you how sorry she is for both of you, for her dead son and for you too, and then she'll cook you a nice dinner and you'll have to eat it, and she'll make you some sandwiches to take in your pocket when you go away. . . ."

What a fine lot of sloppy piffle that is! Hats off! Mother! It's sickening slop. How much better to do as all decent civilized people do. Catch the guilty bastard and murder him too. He had no mercy. Do it legally, of course, and with a fair trial, but shoot him the works like he did to the other fellow. That makes two corpses, and that'll teach 'em that "you can't get away with it." The two corpses sort of balance, keep the scales of justice even, and make us all respect the law. That's the intelligent way to do it, of course. But if you live among crazy people like the Habbe even only for a few weeks, and hear crazy people talk, like old Dounairon, your mind gets all tangled and you begin to have crazy ideas too and to write crazy things afterward.

I thought a good many crazy things while I was living among the Habbe, who are so topsy-turvy and crazy themselves. Take, for instance, all that sex business. I was brought up in Christian communities—in Westminster, Maryland; Abilene, Kansas; Newberry, South Carolina; places like that. If a girl was "ruined" she was ruined, and that was an end of it for her—and often for her family, so far as decent people were concerned, if they didn't move away. As for the girl herself, she had to go away, and all decent people had the satisfaction of knowing that she was rotten from the start, for usually you'd hear afterward that she was in a whorehouse in Baltimore or St. Louis or Atlanta. Sometimes, instead, she tried to have an abortion, or killed her baby and tried to hide it, or didn't try to hide it but just jumped in the creek and drowned herself. At any rate, the community was well rid of her. Of course, for the boys and young men it was different. We had our own whorehouses too, down by the railroad tracks, so that nobody but a traveling salesman or a completely low-down skunk would think of seducing anybody's sister—besides, if he did, her brothers or father would fill him full of lead if he was white, and if he was black it was always rape, of course, and we knew what to do about that. It wasn't a perfect system. There were disadvantages which even the ministers recognized, especially when the minister's son caught gonorrhea or syphilis, as nearly everybody's son did at one time or another. It wasn't exactly perfect. But, by God! we kept our own sisters pure.

And here I was now in a town where the son of the mayor was telling me that when *his* young unmarried sister got knocked up, the neighbors all came and congratulated them, and his mother gave her a party!

People always say that if you spend a little time in an insane asylum, associating with the inmates, even as a visitor, you soon end by getting mixed up and not knowing which are the crazy people and which are the sane ones. Perhaps it was something like this that began to happen to me among the Habbe, for over and over again I kept asking myself ridiculously whether it was they who were really crazy, or whether perhaps we were.

III

SINCE the social and moral customs of any race or group are usually closely interwoven with its religious beliefs and superstitions—and since the customs of these Habbe were so strange—I was anxious above all, if I could, to get at some understanding of precisely what it was that they believed. It was easy to see, and to say, that they had become formal phallic worshipers, relegating their forest Fetichism to a debased and minor rôle. But just what in this case—beyond being, of course, a fertility cult—did phallic worship mean? That wasn't by any means so easy. I had seen their great *toro* altars reared publicly in the sunshine, had learned that the name they called their phallic god was Amma, had even seen libations, flowers, sacrifices on the altars; but as to any real knowledge of the inner meaning of their faith, all this had left me none the wiser.

Endyali said that only a Hogoun, if one could be found who was willing, could explain these matters to me, and that his father was arranging for a visit which we might shortly make to the one most easily available, the Hogoun here at Sangha. He was a dignified old man who received us in his courtyard, in some state, holding a staff surmounted by a carved crocodile's head, white-robed, wearing a tall red hat and high embroidered boots. He was courteous and kindly, but remained wrapped completely in his dignity. I had hoped that he would speak of his god or gods, but he gave me no real confidence, and in answer to my questionings talked only of the outward forms, the ceremonies, the organization of the priestcraft, the letter but not the spirit of their faith. Whatever I learned eventually, and never completely, of the inner meaning of their religion, came later, from a different and higher source. But my contact with the Hogoun of Sangha was not wasted, for I learned at least some curious details concerning the nature of the priestly office and the manner of election to it.

Each separate clan among the Habbe, usually centered in a town, has its own Hogoun, who combines functions somewhat like those of a bishop in religious matters with functions somewhat like those of a supreme court judge in matters concerning the moral conduct and moral welfare of the people. The Hogoun is chosen by a clan council and remains in office for life, but the office is not hereditary. To prepare himself for his functions, he must go through three years of seclusion and mystic contemplation. During this time he can never leave his house,

and the only person he can see is a child, a virgin, who
brings him food. At the end of the three years he loses
his family identity and his family name and becomes
simply the Hogoun of (for instance) Sangha, as we say
the Bishop of Toledo, or the Bishop of San Sebastian.
He is invested with his robes, bonnet, staff of office, and
thereafter lives in a fine house, surrounded by considerable pomp, mystery, and ceremony. He marries, has a
family, numerous servants. In theory, like the Pope of
Rome, he may never set foot on ground or territory that
is not his own or ever enter the house of another; but in
fact he may go where he likes by the simple process of
always wearing special boots when he walks abroad, and
may visit the houses of others preceded by his servants,
who dispose his own rugs, mats, and cushions in the
house which he is planning to honor by his presence, so
that wherever he goes he is considered to be in his own
house. In religious ceremonies the Hogoun presides, but
never himself wields the knife. For this there is a lower
hierarchy, the blood-priests, who come into their priesthood in a much stranger way. Their initiation involves
also a three-year retirement—everything goes by three
with the Habbe—but of a ruder and more savage sort
than that undergone by the Hogoun.

By luck I saw for myself something of what this was
like, since it happened that just at the period of my stay

in Sangha there were somewhere out among the rocks, living in secret caves like savage beasts, or rather as did ancient Christian anchorites and hermit monks in the desert of the Thebaid, two men of Sangha who had been touched by the hand of Amma and who were undergoing this probation for the sacrificial priesthood. Endyali had promised that if ever they approached the town, as they sometimes did, he would let me know and if possible arrange for me to have a glimpse of them. They might run away, he said, on our approach, but at any rate we could try.

One morning he came, saying that they had been seen cultivating an onion patch belonging to the mother of one of them. The onion patch was in a green irrigated hollow about a quarter of a mile from the edge of the town, and as we clambered down over the rocks he told me what he knew of how the hand of Amma descended on such chosen ones. It was even more violent, it appeared, than what had happened to Saul of Tarsus on the Damascus road. Furthermore, he said, it could happen to any man, at any time, without warning. A man might be rich or poor, he said, he might be working in the fields or mending a saddle or sitting in a doorway talking with his neighbors. When the "call" came, the man would first begin to shiver and moan, cover his head with his hands as if to hide or protect himself, then leap up shrieking and howling, tear off his clothes, and rush through the town, out into the waste lands. For three years, he said, the man would live in a cave or in a cleft in the rocks, and during that period could let no razor touch his face. He could not cut his hair, could eat no cooked food, could not sleep in a bed or on a mat or under any roof. However, he could return sometimes to the edge of the town if he wished and could help cultivate the gardens of relatives and could take away with him a handful of onions or a sheaf of grain which he would chew raw—for otherwise, said Endyali, he might completely starve. Great care must be taken, however, when a man of this sort was seen near the town, not to beat any drums, for if he heard drums beating, the frenzy might come on him and he would run away howling. The two we were hoping to see, he told me, were finishing the second year of their probation. We would stop at the spring and take them a calabash of water, and in that way he hoped they would let us approach.

They were bent over, digging peaceably in the onion patch with short wooden hoes, and paid no attention as we came near them. They were naked and emaciated, with long, matted hair and beards. But they seemed as peaceful and normal as any ordinary workers in a garden, and when they looked up and saw us and Endyali saluted them and offered the water, they smiled, returned the salutation, and stopped their work to drink deep. They seemed indeed perfectly normal, and when we went away after a moment—Endyali was afraid we might excite them and be criticized for it afterward in the town—they went tranquilly back to work.

I saw also in Sangha a number of these blood-priests who had finished their initiation and who had been for years engaged in the exercise of their functions. They remained bearded and with long hair, and wore only a coarse short smock belted at the waist with a rawhide leather thong, but were not dirty or disheveled. They were married, lived as other Habbe did, and cultivated their fields.

In early spring, before the rains, at the time of the principal sacrifices to Amma, it was they who cut the throats of the sheep, goats, bulls, and deluged the Priapic obelisks with blood. During other periods of the year they sometimes also, for a small fee, served the Fetichers in the sacrifices to the old idols from the forest.

Endyali knew that while what I wanted chiefly now was to arrive at some sort of clearer comprehension of their great public cult, I was also interested to see what transformations their Fetichism had undergone in being displaced geographically and relegated to a minor rôle. He learned that on a certain day there was to be a Fetich ceremonial at Ireli, a neighboring cliff town, and

suggested taking me to see it. Sangha, as I have badly explained, was on the top of a great palisade. Ireli could
be reached by a short walk, a half hour south, and an
hour or two clambering down the cliff on foot, he said,
but there were ledges and notched ladders which would
be difficult unless one was accustomed; so he suggested
that we go the roundabout way on horseback, through a
tunnel, descending to the plain, and then climbing up
to Ireli, which would be easier.

We decided to go a day early and spend the night
there. Endyali's father gave us horses, and taking no
food because he felt sure we would be welcomed and
well treated, we set out confidently, descended into the
plain, cantered along for three hours through fields at
the foot of the palisades, and came in sight of Ireli.
When I first saw it, it seemed from a little distance that
the whole of the town, with its walls, turrets, terraces,
clung magically to the sheer cliff, but arriving closer and
as the angle changed I could see that it began among the
steep rocks at the cliff's foot, went up gradually from
ledge to ledge, steeper and steeper until finally it did
reach the perpendicular, with terraces, caves, windows,
accessible only by ladders and ropes. Drums were beating
somewhere, high up, but soon after we entered the lower
part of the town they ceased, and the few people we
met in the narrow alleys between the walls and court-

yards of the houses seemed embarrassed, not looking at us frankly. Some of them recognized Endyali and responded to his salutations, but almost as if unwillingly. And when we got to the chief's house where he had expected to be welcomed, entertained, and put up for the night, we were not even invited inside. He had evidently heard of our coming, this chief of Ireli, and it was more than plain to see that we were not welcome. He shook hands and asked after the health of Endyali's father, but he resented me and resented the fact that Endyali had brought me. When asked about the ceremony, he said that it had taken place the week before. He said his house was being repaired—which made no sense at all—and that that was why he couldn't ask us in. The whole trouble, I thought, was my presence. If Endyali had gone alone, he would have been well received. Among blacks in Africa, on their own ground, where there are neither European administrators nor neighboring garrisons, either a white stranger is welcome, or he is not. And if he is not welcome, they have ways, sometimes evasive and sometimes direct, of making him unhappy and getting rid of him, just as painful and efficient as those which white natives employ in America when a Negro wanders into a white restaurant or a white church or tries to find a place to sleep outside the black belt. The chief of Ireli was suavely insulting. When I tried to be conciliating, he was contemptuous and razzed me for my pains. Endyali was getting angry, which was perhaps his right. My resentment was the more painful because, aside from being Endyali's friend, I had no rights there. If they didn't like my white face or didn't want a stranger present at a local religious ceremony, it was after all their own affair, even though he might have been a little more polite about it. But when Endyali said that at any rate, before leaving, he wanted to show me the upper part of the town, and the chief responded bluntly that we couldn't, Endyali was mad enough to fight. He was a free Habbe in a free Habbe town whose ladders and staircases formed free rights-of-way, as our streets do at home. But he was young and indecisive, and there didn't seem to be much that could be done about it. He was ashamed, he said, to have brought me all this way only to be insulted by people of his own tribe, but he didn't have sufficient age or authority to insist against a chief—which was true. In the meantime some villagers, acting, I am sure, under the chief's instructions, because they seemed shamefaced about it, had brought us a scrawny, sickly, starved chicken, not fit for a dog's breakfast, and some dirty eggs, evidently old and surely rotten, saying it was all the food the village had to offer us.

There was nothing to do but go back to Sangha, humiliated and angry. It was a very unpleasant experience and highly illustrative of what can happen to travelers who fall among natives who, for reasons often never completely disclosed, resent their presence.

There was, however, a sequel to this humiliating Ireli adventure, and a partial explanation of it in that some of the older ones in Sangha—everybody heard of what had happened to us, and there was a good deal of talk about it—affected to remember now that this chief of Ireli had an old and personal long-standing spite against whites, dating from some vague injury or injustice he had suffered years before. Be that as it may, when Dounairon Doli learned what had happened, he stormed not only at the chief of Ireli, but at Endyali and me as well, and kept saying to Endyali, "You'll have to go back. You'll have to go back, the both of you. If I weren't bedridden we'd take fresh horses and go immediately. The matter of the ceremony is nothing, but all Ireli people come here freely, and all Sangha people must be free to go where they please in Ireli. We will see what can be done. But you must go back, both of you."

We were ashamed before Endyali's father.

After consulting others, Dounairon decided that the way for us to do it was quietly and in such a manner that if any real quarrel resulted, Ireli would be put in the wrong as the aggressor. The point involved was simply the right of a Sangha man and the guest of a

Sangha man to walk and climb about freely in Ireli. If we returned on horseback to lower Ireli, approaching from the plain, we might be stopped again in the lower town and told that we couldn't climb higher, and if a quarrel started it would be we who had to force it. Dounairon's plan was that we should go on foot instead, descending the cliff by the regular ledges and ladders— and thus we would be directly in upper Ireli. He felt sure, he said, that once there, the chief wouldn't dare order us driven out. But we were to be accompanied by an uncle of Endyali, an older man of force and dignity, who would know what to say if there was a quarrel. All this was not quite so childish and trivial, or so personal to me either as a white man, as it sounds on paper. There was, rather, a question of precedent involved, and of town and family dignity, which Endyali and I, alas, had placed in a feeble, if not actually cowardly, light.

The original trip had taken half a day on horseback, but going down over the edge of the cliff, while difficult, was much quicker. The last half hour of it was goat work, sometimes notched ladders, sometimes ladderlike steps cut in the rock, in one or two places just foot- and hand-holds along ledges worn smooth as marble. For the Habbe it was nothing. Children, old women even, climbed up and down. It wouldn't have been anything, either, for an Alpinist. But having never had any technical experience even as an amateur in real mountain work, there were several moments when I was more afraid of slipping than of any quarrel that might develop on arrival. The uncle helped me, however, carried my shoes strung around his neck, and barefooted I felt safer.

When we got down actually into the inhabited part of the cliff I was so fascinated that I forgot all about being afraid, and about the quarrel too. It was honey-combed with caves, dating evidently from the original troglodytes, which had been improved by the later Habbe, who had built their clay walls and terraces on the ledges. The whole face of the cliff was inhabited like a bee-hive. On almost every terrace and poking their heads from time to time out of cave entrances or little square windows were men, women, children, even dogs. Stopping on a terrace to rest where there were several men sitting and a woman chopping wood, Endyali's uncle sent a man down to tell the chief of Ireli that we were paying a friendly visit to the upper town, and that if by any chance he didn't like it, he could come up and tell him why. Some of the Ireli men who were sitting on the terrace heard the message and laughed. Presently one brought us a jug of water. The uncle explained that I was living in Sangha as a guest of Dounairon's family. They looked at me curiously and talked a great deal, but they were not unfriendly. They were evidently indifferent to their chief's personal grudges and quarrels. Endyali's uncle was known to them, and he knew what to do and say. It was getting hot on the ledge in the sunshine, and presently one of the men invited us to follow him. The ledge we were on was unsheltered, a sort of public place. We climbed some ladders and came to the private terrace of his "house." This terrace was at the wide mouth of a natural cave in the cliffside, with rock overhanging for its roof, and around it had been built a low clay wall, knee high, so that it made a fine, comfortable open veranda, looking out suspended in the air a thousand feet above the immense valley. It seemed a grand way to live—like having a penthouse on a New York skyscraper. This natural porch, opening out toward the valley but protected by its low clay wall and over-hanging roof, was the main living-room of the family in good weather. There were couches covered with skins, a big clay oven, jugs, calabashes, low wooden stools. Carved back artificially into the cliff from this ledge-cave were a number of square chambers, dating evidently from pure troglodyte days. Six people lived there, the man told us, but his women and children were down below just now, in the gardens.

On this terrace, for the first time, I saw a Habbe household altar. The altar itself was a low, flat rectangular stone about two feet wide, not larger. In its center was a phallus molded in clay, standing up like a little post. At the right of it, in a sort of box so that they wouldn't topple over, stood three ugly little wooden dolls not more than six or seven inches tall, little doll-like mario-nettes, their organs rudely sculptured but not exaggerated in size, one male, one female, and one hermaphrodite. At the left of the post was an open bowl containing a blackish liquid, partly coagulated blood, with which the post and the three little idols were smeared. It wasn't pretty, but it was intensely interesting. I asked what sort of ceremonies took place before these family altars. They said no ceremony at all, properly speaking, but that it was the duty of the head of the family to kill a cock from time to time and sprinkle them with the blood that was kept in the bowl. I asked Endyali if families in Sangha had similar altars, and he said no, that it wasn't exactly the same, that many families had given up Fetich-ism entirely and now worshiped only Amma at the public altars. His own family, for instance, he said, had no altar of this sort, but there was preserved at Sangha the ancient Fetich of the Sangha clan, and his family, he said, sometimes sacrificed to it as well as to Amma. Our host, not at all annoyed but rather pleased at our interest in his bloody little gods, took a small cup and sprinkled them with some of the mixture from the bowl, to show how it was done.

Decidedly this second visit to Ireli was more friendly than the first. On that first visit I had noticed, on a terrace, high up and farther to the left than we now were, an object which had seemed to be a big wooden box or ark, brightly painted in striped colors. Before it stood the principal Amma altar of Ireli, and as a matter of cantankerous pride we decided to go there. I felt no embarrassment or compunctions, since Endyali's uncle knew so well what he was about. So we climbed up, no one this time objecting. The chief had never sent back any word at all, nor had he done anything to hinder us. Arriving, we found that the brightly painted ark, which had seemed from down below no larger than a packing-box, was really a square house, large as a family mausoleum or vault in a cemetery, with a big double wooden door, garage-like, closed, but not locked or fastened. There was a sort of caretaker on the ledge, and far from being resentful, he asked—without much interest but expecting a gift, I think—whether we wanted him to open the doors and let us see inside. He was like a sacristan offering to open the door of a crypt or chapel for strangers in Europe. But Endyali's uncle, deciding, I think, that it was Sangha's turn to be contemptuous, said, "No, there's nothing in there worth seeing. We just came up here for a walk along the ledges and to look at the view."

As a matter of fact we had come for no reason at all, except with a chip on our shoulders, to show that we could. I saw the inside of a similar ark later at Aru. It was not a temple but merely a storehouse for the sacred objects, knives, bowls, etc., used in the sacrifices which took place outside on the altar. Needless to say, I never saw any sacrifices at Ireli. When I finally saw a Fetich sacrifice among the Habbe—the Amma sacrifices are as casual, free, and open as our churches are—it came about some weeks later, as such things always come about if they are real, simply by the accident of being present at a family affair among friends in Sangha.

IV

IT WAS a bright sunshiny morning, and we were in the walled backyard of Ogatembili's house. Ogatembili was the chief sorcerer of Sangha, a man I scarcely knew, custodian of Sangha's ancient Fetich.

Endyali's father, Dounairon Doli, head of the Sangha clan, himself continuing sick and unable to be present, had provided a goat and a cock for sacrifice, instructing that prayers be offered for his recovery. There had been some friendly argument the day before with Ogatembili, who saw no special reason for permitting a white person to see the ceremony, but Dounairon had insisted that since the Doli family was paying for the sacrifice and since Endyali and I went everywhere together, I might as well see it as not. Ogatembili didn't really care. By this time everybody knew that I meant no harm, and everybody was either friendly or indifferent to whatever I might do.

It was to be a private family ceremony anyway, and there were only a handful of us present. There was no religious or solemn atmosphere in the preliminary prepa-

290

rations. The yard was inside mud walls ten feet high, but it was nothing but a casual backyard adjoining the house—woodpile, cow-shed, outhouses, the wife and daughter of the sorcerer pounding millet that would be made into a sort of cream to be used in the sacrifice. The goat had been selected the night before from Dounairon's flocks, and stood tethered. A man named Seru, the throat-cutter, a long-haired member of the sacrificial priesthood, in a short brown belted smock, was squatted beside the goat, braiding a new cord. Endyali and I sat on the woodpile, smoking cigarettes, while he explained from time to time why they were doing this or that. The sorcerer was crouched in a corner of the yard with his back to us, holding a red cock between his knees, stroking it and talking to it. Every little while he would toss it free, watch it ruffle its feathers and strut for a moment, then catch it again by a string fastened to one of its feet. Sitting in a backyard on a woodpile and thinking of the magnificent orgiastic chorales and processions by torchlight in the Haitian jungle, with tomtoms booming, and of things I had more recently seen in the Ivory Coast forest, it seemed to me that Fetichism here had fallen to a shabby and sad estate. I had slept badly the night before, for fear they might finally decide not to let me see it after all, but now I didn't care. It is a stupid and self-contradictory fault which I have always had, this wanting to see things as they really are, and then being disappointed. It often crops up in me.

The monotonous preparations went on for nearly half an hour, during which the only thing that happened was that once when the sorcerer tossed the cock from him, it flapped its wings and crowed lustily. Endyali said this was a good omen. At last the women finished preparing the cream of millet—went into the house and shut the door.

The ceremony, whatever it might be, was about to begin. Still no sign of any altar nor of the mysterious Fetich which, Endyali told me, no woman's eye was ever permitted to look upon. That was why we had had to wait until they had finished their task and gone indoors.

At exactly what moment, or why, my boredom gave place to a nervous, unpleasant, half spooky feeling, despite the sunshine and the banal backyard setting, I do not know. Very likely it was nothing more than a nervousness communicated by Endyali, whose explanations were beginning to be whispered and staccato. "They are coming," he said. "They will enter by the gate. You will not be able to see them, but they will be here." "Who will be here?" I asked.

"The old ones who are dead, the ancient guardians of the Fetich." So this was that sort of spirit-stuff, ghost-stuff! Shades of dubious, shabby apartments in Central

Park West where also I had been slightly disgusted and nervous rather than impressed, feeling that if there was really anything supernormal behind the curtains it was something unpleasant and unclean! A prejudgment here, but instinctive, and so not to be controlled.

Ogatembili had opened the gate, a little wooden door it was, in the high wall, and was kneeling just inside the opening with his arms spread wide. The attitude, the gesture, the long white nightgown robe he wore, the tenseness of his face and voice, his heavy breathing, made him seem different from what he had been a little while before.

"Come in," he chanted, "for the moment is now approaching. We are going to offer sacrifice in the old way as you taught us long ago to do, and the reviving blood will flow again for the old forest gods and devils."

When the doubtful ghostly company had trooped in, Ogatembili fastened the gate, and aided by Seru the throat-cutter, opened a small outhouse and dragged from it an immense earthen pot. Then they set up a wooden board, platformlike, on stones, set back in a narrow angle between two outhouses. From the big earthen pot they lifted out the ancient Fetich of the Sangha clan and deposited it on this improvised altar. Endyali had not told me exactly what the Fetich was—the physical, material form of a Fetich may be anything—saying that when the time came I would see for myself. This Fetich was a very old, worm-eaten idol, the carven image of a little man, seated. He wore a crown of shells and snake-vertebrae. He had big ears, a long, almost animal-like muzzle rather than a nose, but the face was human. Tiny *grigris* bags were strung round his neck. He was seated with his hands on his knees. He was barefooted, and though not cross-legged, there was something about the feet and hands and the posture that suggested Buddha. But the face was bestial and he was entirely covered with old clotted blood, streaks black and rotten-reddish, shiny like varnish, and gummy-thick so that you wouldn't want to touch it. I suppose he had been covered with blood like that for generations and centuries. This was his serum "culture," this was what he lived in. He had a tiny bell in his lap. Lying on the board were two iron rings, a sausage-like bag, and an iron knife. These had also come out of the earthen pot and were likewise soaked in old clotted blood.

Ogatembili, kneeling before the Fetich, but lifting his eyes up toward the sky, began a singsong chant, first prudently making his peace with the high, clean God, before devoting his attention to this one. Endyali translated for me in whispers, and I also jotted down phonetically a few of the Habbe phrases.

"*Amma, aganai yaba!*" he repeated. "We salute Thee, Amma, the one, the universal."

Then with sweeping gestures, bowing forward, right, left, backward, and toward the earth, he continued:

"But we salute also those below and those who are round about. We salute you all, gods and devils. There are seven sorts of other gods and we cannot be sure; so we salute you all."

Only after these precautionary invocations did he address directly the little mannikin. He said to it: "We come before you now who protect our family and protect our clan, and who stand between us and those we cannot see. Our business is with you now, and it is you whom we salute.

"I am an orphan, but I bring you salutations from my father and mother. The chief who lies sick offers you a goat and a cock to raise him up and protect him. Behold his son here. Behold also the stranger, but he comes as another son of the chief who lies sick; so protect him also, for he has brought you a bag of cowrie shells. Let him be one who will always march at the head of a procession.

"Behold now, and everything will be done as the ancestors taught us. Behold first the cream of millet."

At this point he arose, sprinkled the idol with the creamy liquid, and poured the rest in libation upon the

board. In the meantime Seru, the throat-cutter, had
led the goat before the altar, with the newly braided
cord.

"Behold now the blood!" chanted Ogatembili, kneeling while the goat was lifted by two assistants and held
so that its throat was immediately above the idol. While
Ogatembili chanted, Seru slashed the throat, so that the
idol and other objects upon the altar were deluged with
wet crimson.

"Behold now the red cock!" chanted Ogatembili, and
why it was that what subsequently followed seemed to
me so horrid and obscene—particularly since I have never
had any clear understanding of what the word "obscene"
means—is a minor personal mystery, not solvable by
reason. For what actually happened was trivial in a
material, physical sense, and no more horrid physically
than what one might see in a Vermont backyard when
the cook is killing and cleaning a chicken for dinner. Yet
it sent sickening shudders through me. I have seen many
blood-sacrifices among primitive peoples, some beautiful
and some with their large element of mystery-horror;
have willingly participated in some of them, have drunk
the blood and been marked with it, and with no feeling
of uncleanness or repulsion. I have seen goats, bulls,
doves slain, fountains of blood flowing while crowds
shrieked and tomtoms boomed, and have liked it on the

whole better than an arid Protestant church service where they merely sing in nasal voices of fountains filled with blood, and I have even reflected that perhaps God might like it better too.

What, then, was happening in this present case?

If any one should ask me whether in my entire life, in all my prying about in far or forbidden places, I had ever seen anything really *horrible*, anything that could send actual shivers down your spine and make your hair stand on end, I think if I replied truly I would say, "Only once, and that was when I saw a chicken sacrificed to a little wooden idol, in broad daylight, in a backyard at Sangha." But when they asked me why it was horrible, I would not be able to explain and they would think I was very silly, for all I could tell about it would be something like this:

"Well, they just cut a chicken's head off and poured the blood on a wooden doll, and then they skinned the chicken's neck, and took the skin from its neck with the feathers on it, and with it made a little cap shaped like a wig which they set askew on the doll's head in place of the little crown of vertebrae it had been wearing. Then they cut off the chicken's comb from the chicken's head, and cut off one of its claws, and took some of the feathers and made a little bouquet which they fastened with string like a little bouquet of flowers for a doll, and they put this in one of the little doll's hands, and then they bowed and capered before it."

"Yes, but what then? What about the horrible thing you were going to tell us?"

"But that was all there was to it—what I have told. That was the end of it. They didn't do anything else. That was the end of the ceremony. They put the doll back in the big earthen jar and put the jar away in the outhouse. And we went away."

V

WE WOULD be leaving the mountains of the Habbe soon, almost surely never to return, and I was unhappy because it seemed to me that I was going away still baffled, still bewildered as I had been during my first days among them.

Concerning their Fetichism, I believed that I now understood at least as much as it is possible to understand with the exterior mind, barring my own emotionally exaggerated inner reactions, which I will not try to analyze. This Fetichism, transplanted from the forest, I thought, and divorced from the mystic conceptions which gave it there a somber power and beauty, divorced also from the animistic beliefs that made it spiritual even in its grossest forms, had here become out of place, a mere degenerate backyard traffic with ugly little minor larvae, hobgoblins, and demons. The Habbe, it seemed to me, played with them and invoked them as civilized Christians play with their indecent dubious mediums, ectoplasms, table-tippings, and "Indian guides"—the same sort of indecent backyard stuff in most cases, if not always.

What I did not understand was the true nature of this public Amma cult which had completely supplanted Fetichism, properly speaking, as a religion. Endyali hadn't been able to make me understand, nor could his father. Outwardly, of course, it was the worship of Priapus. Its symbol was the phallic rod. But it was evidently not merely a sex cult, and I was seeking to apprehend, if I could, what spiritual essence or spiritual concept lay behind the symbol. A Habbe, for instance, coming among us and visiting our public altars, Catholic or Protestant, would see us seeming to worship a cross, a man being tortured, a shiny metal box containing *grigris*, a little white sheep, and a plaster-of-Paris lady dressed up in tinsel and beads like a Spanish grand opera singer in *The Barber of Seville*. But if he returned home without learning what spiritual essences these symbols stood for, he would be as ignorant as when he came. He might have seen, as I had seen here, people visiting the altars, offering their oblations, but it would have left him none the wiser.

"The only person who might give you satisfaction," said old Dounairon Doli, "is the Hogoun of Aru, but he lives far up on another mountain. He never descends, and his house can be reached only by a path which neither horses nor goats can climb. He is the wisest and holiest of all the Habbe. He is in fact the wisest man in the world. Perhaps if you go there he will talk to you, for he receives all who go seeking knowledge of difficult things. I myself have never seen him, but I have a cousin in the town of Aru, and my son can take you to his house with the horses, and afterward my cousin can guide you."

We slept the following night in the cousin's house at Aru. We had been received as members of the family, dining with them at table, sitting on wooden stools; chicken, rabbit, fresh green onions, boiled millet, honey, and millet beer. My bedroom was a warm, dry inner cave carved from the sloping cliffside against which the house was built, and my bed was a carved niche made comfortable with heavy skins laid on straw.

At dawn they awakened me, and led by the cousin, we began our climbing pilgrimage, down across a gorge, then up the tangle of cliffs that piled up into the sky beyond. In ten minutes we were out of sight of Aru, among the steep rocks. There were no ladders, no ropes, no path, no sign of any human habitation. We went bare-footed, not as Moses did because the ground was holy, but because with shoes or boots we'd have slipped off the ledges and broken our necks.

I had been supposing, rather, that the Hogoun of Aru

would be a hermit in a cave. But when we came, after climbing half the morning, to an enormous ledge near the top of the cliff, we found it covered with a considerable agglomeration of walls and buildings. Inside the walls was a stony garden, with a semicircular sunken court and a big stone chair almost like a throne. Stone benches facing it were carved in the cliffside, and facing the garden and the cliff, with its back to the outer walls and the precipice, stood the Hogoun's house, built of clay, but the façade two-storied and pillared like an Egyptian temple, surmounted by a row of phallic cones, and the whole painted in fading polychrome colors with a weather-worn soft pink predominating. In appearance it was more like a temple than a human dwelling, but in actuality it was a sort of episcopal palace rather than either temple or monastery, for however holy the Hogoun of Aru might be, he was not a hermit or a monk, and was very comfortably established and served in his isolation. He had servants who tended his person and cultivated his gardens, a wife, and two young, rather pretty daughters, who were not twins but seemed to be about the same age. The Hogoun himself was not visible. Servants had conducted us through the gate in the outer wall, and now the daughters came out of the house into the garden, full of curiosity, to greet us and offer us water sweetened with honey. The lobes of their ears were bristling with little straws, and they explained that their mamma had just recently pierced them. They laughed about it and said it had hurt, and that all the straws had to be twisted every day. Habbe girls frequently wear as many as a dozen small rings of gold or silver in each ear, and also sometimes wear a jewel in the pierced nostril, as Hindu ladies do. These two girls had nice necklaces, and the tunics they wore were of fine woven material. Evidently the Hogoun of Aru did not regard poverty as a necessary concomitant of holiness.

But when he emerged from the house finally, he himself came bareheaded and barefooted, in an old brown smock such as Count Tolstoi might have worn, and wearing no charms, amulets, or insignia of priesthood or office. He was pure black, tall, of fine and dignified countenance, casual and completely simple in his greetings, but with a faraway look in his eyes, which were also lighted, I thought, with a gentle, kindly humor. He was elderly, strong, slightly patriarchal, though his white beard was only a tiny wisp. He was, so the Habbe believed and had told me, a very wise and holy man, the wisest and holiest in all the mountains and all the world—but he was certainly a simple and kindly one.

He sent his daughters to find us food, and invited the three of us, Endyali, the cousin from Aru, and myself, to sit on the most comfortable of the stone benches, in

the shade. The cousin refused to sit while the Hogoun
was yet standing, and with a smile the Hogoun sat himself down on the bare ground beside the bench. I think
possibly he took a sort of saint's pride and simple vanity
in sitting on the ground there. Or perhaps it was just his
way of making himself perfectly comfortable. He seemed
to like to touch the earth with his hands, and sometimes
fingered his bare feet as a baby does, while he mused and
pondered during pauses in the conversation.

In response to my slowly developed, respectful, and
cautious questions, seeking for whatever esoteric inner
truth and meaning he might be willing to impart concerning the spiritual essence of the Amma cult, he had
said that Amma was not Priapus, nor anything that could
be symbolized materially; Amma, he had said, was God,
the one true universal God.

"But to understand the mystery," he had then continued, "you must understand that *Amma is also Three,
that Amma, unique and indivisible, is yet Three in One.*"

On an almost inaccessible mountain top in the interior
of Africa, among a people who had never heard of Christianity and where missionaries had never penetrated, a
black priest of phallic Amma was pronouncing, or seemed
to be pronouncing, the formula of the Holy Trinity. I
wondered if I had come upon an insoluble mystery like

that of the seeming Christian and Masonic emblems and formulas found in Thibetan monasteries, antedating Christianity itself.

I was to learn from the Hogoun of Aru, however, that despite certain amazing parallels which specialists in the esoteric and occult may care to draw—and they can perhaps do so legitimately, as will be seen—the Holy Trinity of the Habbe was not connected in any outward, literal sense, either theological or historical, with the Christian conception of Father, Son, and Holy Ghost.

Before the Hogoun had pronounced his formula of the Trinity, we had been engaging in a slow conversation, which I think can best be made clear and kept exact by setting down the questions I asked and the answers he made, exactly as I noted them with pencil immediately after our interview.

My question: It is not then the object sculptured in clay upon your altars which you worship?

The Hogoun: Our altars are a symbol of a manifestation of Amma, but we worship only the one true God.

Question: That one universal God is Amma himself?

The Hogoun: There is no other.

Question: In our land we say that we believe also in one universal God, and there are those who claim to have special knowledge of him and to describe him sitting on a great white throne with a great shining countenance, .

this which we teach our children—and to this we raise our altars."

We came down from the mountain. . . . Sea level at Grand Bassam . . . sea level in Marseilles . . . sea level in Paris . . . sea level in New York. . . . Rising from sea level, Eiffel towers, Paramount and Chrysler towers strangely like proud gigantic replicas of Habbe altars, and at their base a people as fantastic and bewildering, even to a man who was born among them, as ever were the Habbe—a people who also seem mad, but who, despite their seeming madness and despite backyard horrors as hideous in their different way as those of Sangha, yet believe too in a religion of life and worship life after their fashion.

THE END

PHOTOGRAPHS
AND MAP

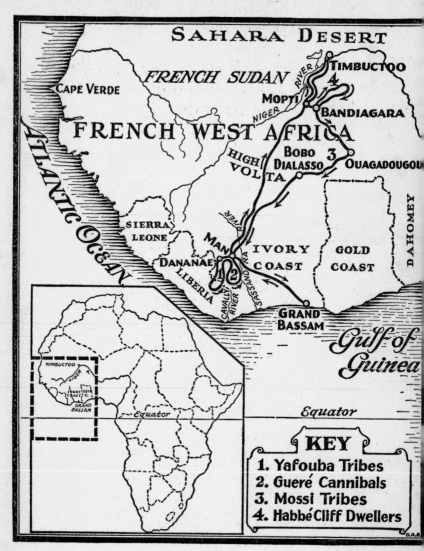

ARROWS INDICATE ROUGHLY, GOING AND RETURNING, THE GENERAL
TERRITORY COVERED BY THE AUTHOR

THE AUTHOR ON THE DANANAE TRAIL WITH THE YOUNG WITCH, WAMBA, WHO BECAME A DOMINATING CENTRAL FIGURE IN HIS ADVENTURES AMONG THE IVORY COAST FOREST PEOPLE. THIS PHOTO WAS SNAPPED BY KLON, THE GREAT APE, THE BUGLER

PORTERS CROSSING THE SUSPENSION BRIDGE OF VINES "CONSTRUCTED
DEMONS AND FIT ONLY FOR APES" WHICH LED ACROSS THE CAVALLY RIVE
INTO THE LIBERIAN HINTERLAND

THE AUTHOR'S "TRAVELING CIRCUS" AT THE COURT OF SAN DEI, THE YAFOUBA CHIEF WHO POISONED HIS BROTHER BOU. THE WHITE WOMAN IS KATIE SEABROOK

YAFOUBA JUGGLER-MAGICIAN WITH ONE OF THE TWO LITTLE GIRLS WHO WERE
TOSSED UPON SWORD-POINTS AND SUPPOSED TO BE MIRACULOUSLY IMPALED

ANOTHER JUGGLER-MAGICIAN AT THE COURT OF SAN DEI. NOTE THE SUPERB
MUSCULAR DEVELOPMENT OF THE ARMS AND TORSO

JUGGLER-MAGICIAN, REVOLVING LIKE A HAMMER-THROWER, PREPARING TO
HURL HIS HUMAN PROJECTILE THROUGH THE AIR

AFTER THE CEREMONY. THE BODY OF ONE OF THE UNINJURED LITTLE GIRLS
WHO IS SUPPOSED TO HAVE BEEN MIRACULOUSLY IMPALED UPON THE SWORDS

MASKED FORTUNE-TELLING WITCH-DOCTOR AT THE COURT OF SAN DEI IN THE IVORY COAST FOREST. AT RIGHT, A SHOUTING "GRIOT," WHO IS INTRODUCING THE MASKED FIGURE

THE LEADING JUVENILE GIRL STAR IN THE BALLET AT SAN DEI'S COURT. THE
MAKE-UP ON HER FACE IS WHITE PAINT

IN THE FOREGROUND, FIVE BOYS RANGING IN AGE FROM NINE TO EIGHTEEN
ADORNED AS GIRLS, AND DOING A FEMALE IMPERSONATION DANCE

A YOUNG YAFOUBA BRIDE-TO-BE ON WHOSE ANKLE THE BLACKSMITH IS WELDING THE IMMENSE
BRASS ANKLET WHICH SHE WILL WEAR ALL HER LIFE

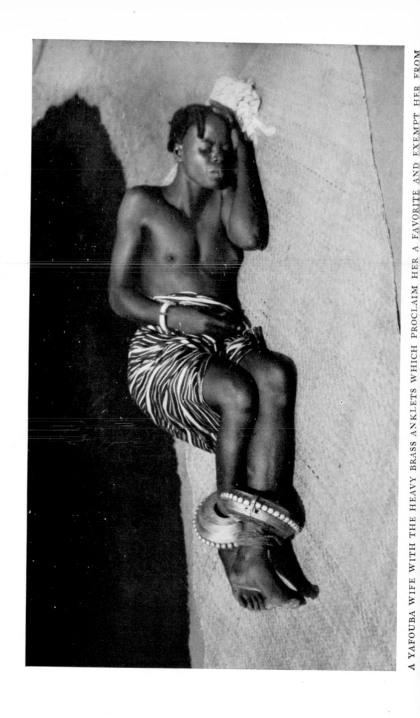

A YAFOUBA WIFE WITH THE HEAVY BRASS ANKLETS WHICH PROCLAIM HER A FAVORITE AND EXEMPT HER FROM

AMONG THE GUERÉ CANNIBALS. SEATED IN THE CENTER, WEARING A METAL FRENCH FIREMAN'S HELMET AND A LEATHER PATCHWORK COAT OF MANY COLORS, IS THE CANNIBAL KING, MON PO, WHO WAS THE AUTHOR'S PRINCIPAL HOST IN THE GUERÉ TERRITORY

A YOUNG GUERÉ CANNIBAL MOTHER IN THE VILLAGE OF MON PO. THE GUE
ARE DESCRIBED BY THE AUTHOR AS THE HANDSOMEST AND FINEST AMONG T
IVORY COAST TRIBES

THIS GENTLEMAN IS THE CHIEF COOK OF THE GUERÉ CANNIBAL TRIBE. HE RE-
SENTED AND DISLIKED ALL WHITES AND POSED FOR THIS PHOTO ONLY BECAUSE
HIS KING INSISTED ON IT

MASKED GUERÉ CANNIBAL WITCH-DOCTOR APPROACHING A VILLAGE WITH RUN-
NERS WHO DRIVE THE WOMEN AND CHILDREN FROM HIS PATH. THIS MASH
HOWEVER, WOMEN AND CHILDREN ARE PERMITTED TO SEE FROM A DISTANC

THE ENTRANCE OF A MASKED WITCH-DOCTOR AT TWILIGHT INTO A GUÉRÉ CANNIBAL VILLAGE. THE RUN-
NER IN THE FOREGROUND HAS A LIGHTED BAMBOO TORCH. THERE IS NO RETOUCHING, AND BECAUSE
OF THE MOVEMENT AND DIFFICULT LIGHT THE AUTHOR REGARDS IT AS THE BEST IN HIS COLLECTION

A GUERÉ WITCH-DOCTOR IN THE MASK OF GLA, THE DEMON. WHEN HE APPEA
ALL THE WOMEN AND CHILDREN ARE DRIVEN INDOORS. HE HAS THE RIGHT
SMITE, AND EVEN KILL, ALL WHO STAND IN HIS PATH. HE AMIABLY POS
FOR THIS PHOTO, AND AFTERWARD ASKED FOR A GIFT

JERÉ WARRIOR WHO HAS JUST BEEN THROUGH A SECRET-SOCIETY RITUAL
IMMUNIZE HIM FROM WOUNDS. CHEWED LEAVES HAVE BEEN SPIT UPON
HIS BODY AND HE HOLDS A LEAF BETWEEN HIS TEETH

A YOUNG GUERÉ APPRENTICE-SORCERESS, KNEELING IN CENTER, UNDERGOIN
A STAGE IN HER INITIATION. SHE SOMETIMES IS FORCED TO REMAIN KNEELIN
FOR AN ENTIRE DAY AND NIGHT

PROACHING TIMBUCTOO. THE YATANGA NABA, HEREDITARY SPIRITUAL
JLER OF THE MOSSI TRIBES. IT IS SAID THAT IF HE EVER LOOKS UPON THE
ACE OF HIS COUSIN, THE MORO NABA, TEMPORAL RULER, ONE OF THEM
WILL DIE

A TYPICAL STREET IN TIMBUCTOO. THE EXTERIOR IS LIKE AN EGYPTIAN CE-
ETERY, BUT INSIDE THE HOUSES AND ON THEIR ROOFS, A RICH AND INTE
ESTING LIFE GOES ON

THE FAMOUS AUGUSTINIAN MONK, PÈRE DUPUIS-YAKOUBA, WHO QUIT HIS
ROBES TO BECOME THE GREATEST LIVING AUTHORITY ON NATIVE LANGUAGES
AND CUSTOMS IN FRENCH WEST AFRICA. HE IS TIMBUCTOO'S LEADING CITIZEN

SALAMA, THE BELOVED AND ESTIMABLE NATIVE WIFE OF PÈRE DUPU
YAKOUBA, FIRST LADY OF TIMBUCTOO, WHO HAS GIVEN HIM THIRTY SO
AND DAUGHTERS

IN TOPSY-TURVY LAND, THE COUNTRY OF THE HABBE. A CORNER OF IRELI, A
TOWN BUILT PARTLY AMONG THE ROCKS AND PARTLY ON THE PERPENDICULAR
CLIFF

HABBE DANCERS WITH STYLIZED MASK HEADDRESSES SYMBOLIZING THE CROC-
ODILES AND OTHER ANIMALS CONNECTED WITH THEIR LEGENDARY ANCESTRAL
HISTORY

HABBE DANCERS WITH MASKS OF GRASS-NET AND COWRIE SHELLS, REPRESENTING THE ENEMIES WITH WHOM THEIR ANCESTORS FOUGHT IN ANCIENT TIMES

THE PUBLIC CHILDREN'S ALTAR AT SANGHA. LITTLE BOYS BRING LIBATIONS AND WILD FLOWERS TO THE
CLAY-SCULPTURED PHALLIC REPRESENTATION OF THE MALE GENERATIVE ORGAN

THE HOLIEST MAN (OR SO IT WAS SAID) IN WEST CENTRAL AFRICA. HE LIVES ON A HIGH MOUNTAIN AND HAS SEEN ONLY THREE WHITE FACES. THE HOGOUN OF ARU IN HIS COURTYARD